Mrs M Maclarty
4 Balvaird
Muir Of Ord
Ross-Shire
IV6 7RQ

D1485649

To, My Parents.
From, George.

New Year. 1990

THE ART OF LIFE

The Art of Life

EDITH SCHAEFFER

Compiled and edited by
LOUIS GIFFORD PARKHURST, JR.

KINGSWAY PUBLICATIONS
EASTBOURNE

Text copyright © Edith Schaeffer 1987
Illustrations copyright © Floyd E Hosmer 1987

First published in the USA by Crossway Books
a division of Good News Publishers, Westchester, Illinois

First British edition 1988

Biblical quotations are from the New International Version
© International Bible Society 1973, 1978, 1984
Published by Hodder & Stoughton

Cover painting by Floyd E Hosmer in a design by Karen L Mulder
Interior design by Floyd E Hosmer and Karen L Mulder

British Library Cataloguing in Publication Data

Schaeffer, Edith
   The art of life.
   1. Christian life – Devotional works
   1. Title
   242
        ,

   ISBN 0-86065-642-X

Printed in Great Britain for
KINGSWAY PUBLICATIONS LTD
Lottbridge Drove, Eastbourne, E Sussex BN23 6NT by
Richard Clay Ltd, Bungay, Suffolk
Reproduced from the original text by arrangement with
Crossway Books

Contents

An Appreciation
by Catherine Marshall[1]

*T*he God I know does not want us to divide life up into compartments–"This part is spiritual, so this is God's province, but that part over there is physical, so I'll have to handle that myself." If we are to believe Jesus, His Father and our Father is the God of all life, and His caring and provision include a sheepherder's lost lamb, a falling sparrow, a sick child, the hunger pains of a crowd of four thousand, the need for wine at a wedding feast, and the plight of professional fishermen who toiled all night and caught nothing. These vignettes, scattered through the Gospels like little patches of gold dust, say to us, "No creaturely need is outside the scope or range of prayer."

The experience of Edith and Francis Schaeffer beautifully illustrates how material, physical, and spiritual needs are all part of a whole. I first became aware of this couple through reading Francis Schaeffer's *The God Who Is There* in 1971, followed by Edith Schaeffer's *L'Abri*.

In August 1953, Francis Schaeffer became convinced that God was calling him and his family to a higher level of giving, working, and sacrifice; to give up the security of a fixed income for an uncertain, nonstructured work in Europe, possibly with a Swiss base.

After reading Edith Schaeffer's account of all this and pondering it, what interested me was that as the Schaeffers

[1]Abridged from Chapter Eleven of *Something More* by Catherine Marshall, copyright © 1974 by Catherine Marshall LeSourd, published by Chosen Books, Fleming H. Revell Company. Used by permission.

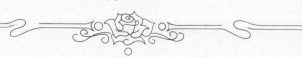

moved on to that higher level of obedience and commitment, God's supply started to work in their lives in a different way—what I choose to call supernaturally. I wondered if I wasn't glimpsing an important principle here.

With a wife and four children to provide for, Dr. Schaeffer knew that this had to be a family decision and a family commitment. As the spiritual head of his home, Francis Schaeffer laid out before his wife Edith and their children all the alternatives. The decision was unanimous—they would say "Yes" to God's call and depend on Him to supply the $1800 the six of them needed for the boat fare to Europe. However, circumstances had created a deadline; if the Schaeffers were to go, they would have to have all of the $1800 in just three weeks, by September 9th when the boat sailed.

Their daughter Priscilla painted a big thermometer on a poster. Within a few days the poster was beginning to show a red line depicting the money received. Opening the mail became the most exciting event of each day. Checks began arriving from the most unexpected sources, most of them for small amounts. The red line on Priscilla's thermometer kept rising. God was giving the Schaeffers a foretaste of what was to become a way of life for this family—trusting the "God who is there" to supply whatever they needed.

In those days of late August and early September 1953, God the Person replied. During the three weeks all of the $1800 arrived. It was the opening door to the work that became L'Abri (meaning "the shelter"), a Christian evangelical community in the tiny village of Huemoz high in the Swiss Alps.

In reading *The God Who Is There* I had been intrigued by two strong features of Dr. Schaeffer's approach not usually found in the same person: he is a conservative, committed evangelical who stands upon all the major tenets of the Christian faith, yet his appeal is to the intellect rather than to the emotions.

In August of 1972, my husband Len and I flew from New York to Geneva, planning to go on to see the Schaeffers. The Schaeffers seemed to be living in God's

kingdom using the coin of that realm. I was eager to see with my own eyes what the coin was and how it worked.

By the time we reached Ollon, the road had begun to climb. Suddenly we were in the tiny remote village of Hue-moz. All around us were sparkling sunshine and brilliant flowers cascading from balconies and windows of Alpine chalets. A sharp turn up a steep driveway and we were at Chalet les Melezes.

It was a surprise to see that Dr. Schaeffer, born an American, had become so European in appearance, rather like some philosopher-hermit out of the Middle Ages. Not a tall man, his gray hair is casually cut and he wore a trim gray goatee. Kindly intelligent brown eyes dominated his face. He was fond of wearing baggy Swiss tweed knicker-bockers, long woolen socks, and brogue-type shoes that should by all rights have been ornamented by a silver buckle.

Edith Schaeffer was a more vivacious, gregarious version of her philosopher-husband. Her mind, her speech, and her body seemed ceaselessly active. As individualistic as her hus-band, she wore her long dark hair combed straight back, loosely twisted into a chignon. More often than not she was a study in browns—her deep brown eyes set off by one of the brown dresses she is fond of wearing.

Our first few hours at L'Abri provided the initial clue as to how God provides material resources for those living in His kingdom on earth: the Schaeffers' part was a total self-giving with every inch of space, every scrap of food, every last franc, every quarter-hour and vestige of strength. Dr. Schaeffer still had no office, nowhere to work privately ex-cept the bedroom. It is a rare night one finds no youngsters sleeping on Mrs. Schaeffer's kitchen floor.

Why had God chosen to ask this of the Schaeffers—and then proceeded to supply their every need? Here is the heart of their prayer-miracle of supply: they could ask and confidently expect *because they had given everything in advance.* After a few hours at L'Abri, one realizes that Edith and Francis Schaeffer have long since laid everything on the altar, even their privacy.

Why? In Dr. Schaeffer's words, "What we seek supremely here in the L'Abri community is to exhibit in some poor fashion the love of God and the holiness of God simultaneously in the whole spectrum of life."

Even in our short visit Len and I felt God's love as all feel it at L'Abri. We sensed Edith and Francis Schaeffer's deep concern and interest in the young people, especially the hippies and the floaters. They care passionately, totally, with utter self-giving about those who don't know what to believe, who have lost their way in life. That there is truth to be found in the Scriptures, that God will see to it that we have that truth—that is the fire in their souls, the light in their eyes, the ring in their voices.

Exhibiting the love of God in the whole spectrum of life.

Introduction

Edith Schaeffer's warm loving smile and bright brown eyes bespeak the heart of hospitality beating strongly within her. If you knock at the door of any L'Abri "shelter" around the world, you will be met with the understanding that *you* may be one of God's divine interruptions in the midst of a very full hour or day, reflecting the attitude Edith models for every Christian.

A bundle of unequaled explosive physical, mental and spiritual energy, Edith strives to make herself captive to the love of Christ–that every ounce of her strength might be used for God's glory and the benefit of others. When limp with exhaustion, trying to live at the age of seventy-two as though she were thirty-six, she often calls upon the Holy Spirit to give her the power to carry on when yet another demand, obligation, or call to obedience beckons.

Intensely practical and multitalented, she can discuss the most profound human concerns while peeling onions in her kitchen or making little sandwiches for high tea. Capable of doing many things at once, she can draw a cartoon-like illustration for little children in their pews to explain the pastor's sermon as he is preaching. Concerned for the ministry of God's beauty to the soul, candles and flowers along with high tea or an evening concert in her home have become her trademark. Or perhaps we should picture her taking a bowl of lovely fresh fruit to someone in affliction, along with reminding them of the comfort in the Scriptures, as the "cup of cold water" for the thirsty.

Her writings of over thirty years in *L'Abri Family Letters* and eleven books bear the stamp of the practical Christian concern, comfort, and compassion which characterizes not only her life, but the God she worships and serves. She applies the truth of God's Word, the Bible, to the whole of life–to every situation and with every person. She endeavors to maintain an open and clear channel of communication to

God, her Heavenly Father, so Christ, His Son, can reach down through her to those hurting and dying in our world. She practices prayer; and by living the truth of God, she gives strength and encouragement to others even when their particular trials or afflictions cannot be removed. She demonstrates that the need for food, shelter, clothing, or proper medical attention for the needy concerns every Christian, in addition to giving them true truth as the basis for daily living.

Having known Edith and Francis Schaeffer since their coming to Rochester, Minnesota, in 1978, for treatment of Francis Schaeffer's cancer at Mayo Clinic, I know that Edith's words over the years have not been empty sounds. She has not just spun out hopeful theories to give people meaning in troubled times. She has based her life on the absolute truth and the objective revelation of God in the Bible, and she has shared her knowledge and understanding with the needy around the world. When the very severe personal blow came to her and to her husband in 1978–"you have cancer, and possibly six weeks to six months to live"–her faith held her steady, and God in Christ gave them both the strength and encouragement to keep on. Dr. Schaeffer died in May of 1984, but Edith still carries on an extensive writing and lecturing ministry built on the foundation of the Scriptures and a living faith in Jesus Christ as Lord and Savior.

The selections from her eleven books in these thirty-one devotions have been carefully chosen to provide a continuity of thought in Biblical teaching. Each of her books builds upon the ones before, and I have tried to put these devotions in an order that will enable the truths she has to offer to build upon one another. Each devotional presupposes that you have read the ones before; otherwise, this first book of her devotions could degenerate into simply a series of unconnected "positive statements in the midst of an absurd situation." Edith Schaeffer carefully builds her positive and encouraging words on the foundation of "the God who is there, and who is not silent" and in the context of the nature of our world, the present condition of the human

race and its destiny, and why we have the problems we face. This first collection of her devotions, selected from her works, had to have the context she herself has so carefully worked to preserve and explain over the years. The first nine devotions are particularly foundational for all that follows. To explore further the thoughts and ideas that intrigue you or meet your particular need, you should read the book from which the meditation is selected. A bibliography of her books will be found at the back of this book.

In addition to selecting and compiling the meditations from her works, I have chosen an appropriate Scripture reading to begin each day's devotional. I have concluded each devotional with a personal prayer that you may choose to make your own; however, I would encourage you to further meditate upon what Edith teaches and personally apply her ideas to your own concerns in prayer to the Person who is not mechanical in His relationship with us. You may use the personal notes page at the end of each devotion to record your reflections and daily growth.

I have used the *New International Version* throughout this book, and have substituted this version for the various versions Edith used from book to book. Prior to the publication of the *New International Version,* both she and Dr. Schaeffer used the *King James Version.* I have included the Scripture references in the text of the meditation, whether or not Edith did this in the original version. In editing the text of her work, I have standardized the various house rules for the copy editing done by her different publishers; for example, I have capitalized the pronouns referring to God, something that has varied from publisher to publisher and even in later books of the same publisher. I have a theological reason for doing so, and also believe it makes for a clearer understanding of the text. I chose not to use . . .'s or —'s to show any ellipses between sentences or paragraphs. I decided not to show within the text any omissions of words, sentences, paragraphs or pages, because this would interfere with your devotional reading. Most of us would be continually tempted to ask, "I wonder what he left out here?" and miss the meaning of what the devotional is

trying to convey. Only on rare occasions have I rewritten a sentence; that usually to ease a transition between paragraphs. Since all of her books are in print and readily available, you may seek further expansion of her thoughts by referring to the pages in her books listed in the footnotes following each day's devotional reading.

I would like to thank Edith Schaeffer for her encouragement in pursuing this project, and for trusting me to compile and edit materials that should represent her work fairly and be of most help to her readers. I would like to thank Dr. Lane Dennis for his encouragement to do this work for Crossway Books from the very conception of the idea and my discussions with him. Floyd and I also wish to thank Mary Lou Sather for all her very valuable editorial advice, assistance and encouragement in the preparation of this book. Edith Schaeffer has entrusted both of us with a project that we hope will minister to many people who have never known her writings before, be a book people can give to meet the needs of those they are trying to serve in various ways, and be a devotional book people who know and love her will enjoy. Finally, I wish to thank Floyd Hosmer for the beautiful art throughout this book. Floyd is an artist practicing fine art and medical illustration in Rochester, Minnesota. He has been a faithful friend of the Schaeffers for several years. Floyd and I appreciate the staff of Crossway Books for giving us the opportunity to be a part of their creative design team in the production of this book. We hope this book will be a lasting heirloom, and a tribute to the work of Edith Schaeffer. Our Heavenly Father has helped us blend together many ideas, and made this book a joy to compile and illustrate. We hope you will rejoice in God as you use this book in your quiet times.

May this book give you strength in affliction, truth in doubt, encouragement to keep on, faith in our Lord Jesus Christ.

For the sake of His Kingdom,
L. G. Parkhurst, Jr.
August 1986

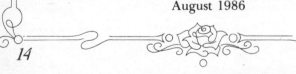

The Art
of Life

ONE

*"In the beginning was the Word,
and the Word was with God,
and the Word was God. He was
with God in the beginning.
Through him all things were
made; without him nothing was
made that has been made."*

John 1:1-3

God, the Artist

*T*he only artist who is perfect in all forms of creativity–
in technique, in originality, in knowledge of the past
and future, in versatility, in having perfect content to express as well as perfect expression of content, in having
perfect truth to express as well as perfect expression of
truth, in communicating perfectly the wonders of all that
exists as well as something about Himself–is of course
God, the God who is Personal.

God, the Artist! We read in the New Testament: "For
by him *all* things were created: things in heaven and on
earth, visible and invisible" (Colossians 1:16, italics added).

God's art communicates! We are told in the Old Testament: "The heavens declare the glory of God; the skies
proclaim the work of his hands. Day after day they pour
forth speech; night after night they display knowledge.
There is no speech or language where their voice is not
heard. Their voice goes out into all the earth, their words
to the ends of the world" (Psalm 19:1-4). In these words we
learn that the whole of creation *communicates* something.
More of creation can now be inspected as man brings some
of the moon rock back with him; more can be seen
through a telescope or with the naked eye. All that we see
in the stars and the planets, in the sun and the moon, are
not only there for useful reasons, but also as an art form, a
communication of the glory and the greatness of the Artist. They communicate the wonder of who He is, and what
was in His mind as He created: not *all* of what was in His
mind, but something *truly* of what was in His mind.

The heavens continue to declare to us something of the
fact that God is there. They testify that He exists, that He
is the Supreme Artist and the Perfect Scientist, who created the moon, and who made the universe so precise in its
composition and detail that man can calculate with complete accuracy where two spaceships will meet in the

depths of space. Why the precision of our calculations? Simply because the precision is *there*—it has been created by the precise God. The heavens declare His glory: they *continue* to declare His glory.

The men of history, the people of all the centuries of human existence, have had before their eyes evidence of the Artist in whose mind these ideas first took shape, and who was able to express them in a visible form. God gave man a mind that could logically work out that the heavens are declaring something, are communicating something: they are speaking of the glory of the Person who made them. "For since the creation of the world God's invisible qualities—his eternal power and divine nature—have been clearly seen, being understood from what has been made, so that men are without excuse" (Romans 1:20).[1]

For Further Reading: Psalm 89, Proverbs 1, Mark 1

PRAYER

Dear Father, thank You for creating a world that declares not only the beauty of Your handiwork, but also the beauty of Your character. You have created a world that is precise, like a dependable machine, and also a world that shows those qualities of Your personality that appreciate true artistic beauty. Everything You have made appeals to my personality in such a way that I am drawn beyond myself to look toward the One who has created me. The heavens declare Your glory to me, and they call me to love not only their beauty, but the beauty of the One who created the stars in the sky and the circling planets around the sun. Thank You for making Yourself known to all people through the world You have made, for Jesus' sake. Amen.

[1] From *Hidden Art*, pp. 14-18.

PERSONAL NOTES

TWO

*"In the beginning God created
the heavens and the earth. . . .
God created man in his own
image, in the image of God he
created him; male and female
he created them. . . . God saw
all that he had made, and it
was very good."*

Genesis 1:1, 27, 31

A Personal Creation

*M*y husband often says there are only two possible beginnings to the universe. He says the third one would be "nothing nothing" to start with, which boggles the human mind too much to accept.

He puts it like this: "Either the universe had a personal beginning, or an impersonal beginning. The universe is therefore either an impersonal universe, or a personal one. If it is an impersonal universe, the evolvement of personality is a sad thing, because there is no satisfactory explanation giving meaning to thinking, acting, communicating, loving, having ideas, choosing, being full of creativity, and responding to the creativity of others. It is like a fish developing lungs in an airless universe. The longings and aspirations of personality drown without fulfillment."

If one chooses the impersonal beginning, one must go on to a logical conclusion of an impersonal universe, and an insignificant human being, and a meaningless history.

However, there *is* Someone at home in the universe. There is Someone to look up to. There is a light in the darkness. There is a door in the wall. There is *truth* to be found. There is another possibility of another kind of beginning. Beginning at this other beginning, there is another end!

It is necessary to start with the first book of Moses. "In the beginning God." That is to say, in the beginning a Person—an Infinite Person, but truly a Person. In the beginning thinking, acting, feeling, love, communication, ideas, choice, creativity. Yes, in the beginning this God who made man in His image. Personality already existing. A personal universe created by a Person. A "people-oriented universe" created by a Person. A universe with fulfillment in it for the aspirations of artists, poets, musicians, landscape gardeners, because it has been created by an Artist, Poet, Musician, Landscape Gardener. Man made in the

image of One who is a Creator—so that man is made to be creative. Bach, Beethoven, Tolstoy, Leonardo da Vinci—not accidental arrangements of molecules by chance creating, but men made in the image of God who are *amazing* because they are men with capabilities of both appreciating what other people create, and of creating themselves in a variety of areas. Compassion not suddenly appearing out of nowhere, but compassion already there in the One who made man in His image.

If you come to realize that the universe must have had a personal beginning, that it really is a people universe, you breathe a sigh of great relief when you discover that a verbalizing God, able to communicate with the verbalizing people He created, has put into understandable words the account we need to know concerning the beginning.

Moses was given by inspiration the understanding and factual knowledge to impart in words to those who would follow, as he told what God told him, "In the beginning God."[1]

For Further Reading: Psalm 143, Proverbs 2, Mark 2

PRAYER

Dear God, thank You for creating me in such a way that I can look at the universe and at the way I am made and see that You are there and that You are a personal God. Everything around me declares that I do not live in a universe that came into existence and maintains its existence on the basis of time plus chance. Thank You for speaking to me in the Bible. Thank You for communicating to me that my eyes and my mind do not deceive me when I place my faith in Your existence with good and sufficient reasons based upon my observations of the world around me. You are indeed a wonderful God to lead me in the light instead of leaving me in the dark. In Jesus' name, Amen.

[1] From *Christianity Is Jewish*, pp. 17-25.

PERSONAL NOTES

THREE

*"When I consider your heavens,
the work of your fingers, the
moon and the stars, which you
have set in place, what is man
that you are mindful of him, the
son of man that you care for
him? You made him a little
lower than the heavenly beings
and crowned him with glory
and honor."*

Psalm 8:3-5

Artwork and Artist

*M*an was made *in the image of God*. But what is God like? In whose image is man made? Certainly, he is made in the image of a Person, so man is a person. God has all the marks of personality, so man is a personality, who can think, act and feel. Therefore man loves, because he has been given the capacity for love. He has been made in the image of One who has loved for ever and ever. (The Father has loved the Son and the Holy Spirit. The Son has loved the Father and the Holy Spirit. The Holy Spirit has loved the Father and the Son.) Man can communicate because he was made in the image of God who communicates within the Trinity. Man has a capacity for communicating and receiving communication, for sharing with other human beings and also with God. But the heart of the discovery is this: we are created in the likeness of *the Creator. We* are created in the image of a *Creator.*

So we are, on a finite level, people who can create. Why does man have creativity? Why can man think of many things in his mind, and choose, and then bring forth something that other people can taste, smell, feel, hear and see? Because man was created in the image of a Creator. Man was created that he might create. It is not a waste of man's time to be creative. It is not a waste to pursue artistic or scientific pursuits in creativity, because this is what man was *made* to be able to do. He was made in the image of a Creator, and given the capacity to create—on a finite level of course, needing to use materials already created—but he is still the creature of a Creator.

But in creativity choice is involved. Why were we not made so that we could not do anything but *one* set of things which would have been absolutely good and without sin? We were to have choice so that *love would have meaning*. Love could have no meaning without choice. (We would not wish to be loved by a robot that has been pro-

grammed to love us.) But more than that is involved. Something that is not mentioned very frequently by people speaking of the problem of "choice"–and agonizing over why man had to have choice anyway, because of all the sorrow of sin and suffering–is one of the most central things involved in the principle of choice, and that is *creativity*. Creativity *involves* choice.

What is creativity? What is it we do when we create something? We start with an idea, or a number of ideas. Something comes into our minds. We have a flow of ideas, sometimes a tremendous flow of ideas, at times in one direction, or at other times in another direction, or perhaps even ten directions at once. *And we have to make a choice.* We cannot do everything that comes into our minds.

Man has a capacity both for responding and producing, for communicating as well as being inspired. It is important to respond to the art of others, as well as to produce art oneself. It is important to inspire others to be creative as well as to communicate by one's own creative acts.[1]

For Further Reading: Psalm 102, Proverbs 3, Mark 3

PRAYER

Dear Father, when You created me, when You created the universe in which I live, You had before You many different possibilities and choices You could have made. I thank You for creating the universe as You have created it, and I thank You for choosing to create me and all humans in Your image. Thank You for giving us personalities with the ability to love and create–to make choices for beauty instead of ugliness in things we create as well as in relationships. Help me to make right choices today. Help me to inspire others to use their talents creatively for You and those You have created to enjoy life and beauty. Amen.

[1] From *Hidden Art,* pp. 23-25.

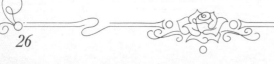

PERSONAL NOTES

FOUR

"What good is it, my brothers, if a man claims to have faith but has no deeds?"

James 2:14.

Conscious Discipline

*I*t seems to me that the marks of personality–love, communication, and moral sensitivity–which are meant to sharpen as we are returning to communication with God, should lead to an *increased* rather than a decreased creativity. The Christian should have more vividly expressed creativity in his daily life, and have *more* creative freedom, as well as the possibility of a continuing development in creative activities.

Christians have a capacity for spiritual communication with God. So we need to spend adequate time with Him, reading His communication to us and praying in intercession for others, and for our own needs. And of course we are limited by finiteness and our time is precious. Of course, Christians have a responsibility to communicate truth to others who do not know it. These are all priorities; and such aspects of a healthy, growing Christian life cannot be ignored or contradicted when we are practicing creative endeavors.

All art involves conscious discipline. If a person is going to paint, do sculpture, design a building or write a book, it will involve discipline in time and energy–or there would never be any production at all to be seen, felt, or enjoyed by others.

A Christian, above all people, should live *artistically, aesthetically, and creatively.* We are supposed to be representing the Creator who is there, and whom we *acknowledge* to be there. It is true that all people are created in the image of God, but Christians are supposed to be *conscious* of that fact, and being conscious of it should recognize the importance of living artistically, aesthetically, and creatively, as creative creatures of the Creator. If we have been created in the image of an Artist, then we should look for expressions of artistry, and be sensitive to beauty, responsive to what has been created for our appreciation.

Does this mean that we should all drop everything to concentrate on trying to develop into great artists? No, of course not. But it does mean that we should consciously do *something* about it. There should be a practical result of the realization that we have been created in the image of the Creator of beauty. Whether you are married and have a family; whether you share a house or a flat with one or a number of people; whether you still live with your parents; whether you live alone and have guests in from time to time; whether you are a man or a woman: the fact that you are a Christian should show in some practical area of a growing creativity and sensitivity to beauty, rather than in a gradual drying up of creativity, and a blindness to ugliness. I believe strongly that the suppressing of hidden artistic talents or appreciation has the effect of warping us as personalities.[1]

For Further Reading: Psalm 9, Proverbs 4, Mark 4

PRAYER

Dear Father, I confess that I have not led the disciplined life I could have led. I am conscious of not using the natural talents and abilities You have given me, and I confess that I have not consciously asked the Holy Spirit to enhance my capabilities for the sake of Your Kingdom and other people. I resolve today to look at the many gifts You have given to me, and I pray that You will help me to make wise choices in how I will use those gifts in creative ways to bring beauty into my world and really communicate to others that I am a creature made in the image of a wonderful and loving Creator. Amen.

[1] From *Hidden Art*, pp. 29-33, 107.

PERSONAL NOTES

FIVE

*"The Lord God took the man
and put him in the Garden of
Eden to work it and take care
of it. And the Lord God
commanded the man, 'You are
free to eat from any tree in the
garden; but you must not eat
from the tree of the knowledge
of good and evil, for when you
eat of it you will surely die.'"*

Genesis 2:15-17

Choices Have Consequences

We have not been given a poetic aspirin pill with which to jump out of reality into fantasy. We have been given history and the intelligence to listen to that history and understand our present dilemma.

Moses wrote what God gave him knowledge to write as he tells us that all things were made good, and that man made in God's image had a place of dominion over the fish of the sea, the birds of the air, and the animals of the earth.

Adam and Eve were given the marvelous garden, landscaped for them by the Gardener who also created the plants in the first place, and who came to talk with them evening after cool evening, at the end of perfect day after perfect day: the Garden of Eden–Paradise that was to be lost.

Evil is not an impersonal bowl of something that spilled out into the world. Evil is a matter of choice, and that choice has to take place in a rational mind. Sin is first in the realm of mind, and then takes place in actions. There is a tremendous choice involved in Lucifer's saying, "I *will* exalt my throne above the stars of God. I *will* ascend into heaven. I *will* be like the most High" (see Isaiah 14:12-17). The plan to lead an aggressive attack against the Triune God and the faithful loyal angels was the first battle plan, the first war. This war still continues, and all other wars have some relationship to it. It was not an impersonal chance happening that this angel revolted and drew others into the revolt: it was an act of the will.

The reality of a personal universe is seen not only in the creation we observe, feel, taste, hear, but in the constant evidence within us of this struggle: "To do or not to do, that is the question." We have a choice to make moment by moment, we *know* we have choice. We can be told we are a chance collection of molecules making us into machines, but our experience cuts across this, and people

crash their heads into the reality of the choices affecting their own lives, the choices they even deny exist: to do or not to do.

After God's creation of Adam and Eve, and His constant communication with them, Lucifer, now Satan, came and spoke to Eve saying, "Did God really say, 'You must not eat from any tree in the garden'?" (Genesis 3:1). A subtle injection of doubt into Eve's mind. Satan implied that perhaps God had not spoken the truth.

Satan is not very original. His subtle question is really the same through the centuries, and in this century. Every human being who has ever heard or read the words in the Bible hears Satan's question at one time or another: "Did God really say this? Is this really the Word of God? Can you trust this as being truth? Or____?" He implants the doubt that is the forerunner of denial that God's communication to man is true truth.[1]

For Further Reading: Psalm 55, Proverbs 5, Mark 5

PRAYER

Dear God, thank You for making every person a significant person: people who can make choices that have real consequences. Thank You for showing us through Adam and Eve that You respect the decisions we make, as horrible as their decision to disobey You was and has been for the world You created. Help me to think things through and realize that You would never lie to me or do anything from a selfish motive. You can be trusted absolutely. Help me to believe Your Word, the Bible, even when there are portions that I cannot fathom with my finite brain, because I know You, the Author. By Your Holy Spirit, guide me and guard me so the choices I make will have good consequences for others as well as myself, for Jesus' sake. Amen.

[1] From *Christianity Is Jewish,* pp. 27-31

PERSONAL NOTES

SIX

"The Lord saw how great man's wickedness on the earth had become, and that every inclination of the thoughts of his heart was only evil all the time. The Lord was grieved that he had made man on the earth, and his heart was filled with pain."

Genesis 6:5

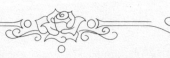

God's Art Museum

*H*ave you ever been through an art museum after it was vandalized? Have you ever seen a beautiful home after vandals got through with it? Have you come back to a place you yourself made beautiful right after violent, senseless vandals had slashed it up? Perhaps then you have a very small understanding of the necessity to explain to people in words something of what you expect to do as you restore the devastating destruction, and as you promise to them that they will be amazed when they see it.

Perhaps you have restored paintings, maybe that is your profession. Perhaps you have restored old furniture, ruined by people who don't appreciate antiques. Maybe then you have the background, having been made as a person in the image of a Person, to begin to have some understanding of destruction of what has been made, and the need of a solution so that there may be a restoration.

Adam and Eve rushed ahead to eat of the tree of the knowledge of good and evil, believing Satan rather than God, and plunging themselves, and the generations to follow them, into darkness. Death has now entered the universe. Death is separation. Adam and Eve were separated from communication with God. Their perfect relationship with each other was spoiled, and separation of person from person began. Separation psychologically of the person inside had its beginning. Separation of body and soul was ahead for them, but disease and physical pain and brokenness began. The universe became abnormal. Satan had walked through God's "art museum"–that is, the artwork of God's hands–and had vandalized it with slashes of senseless destruction, trying to separate people from God, and in his declared battle he planned to continue this drive to separate people from God, with seemingly endless lies to contradict true truth in a variety of ways. Satan and his followers were to have a certain length of time before the

end of this rebellion would come. We are still in that period of time before the end.

God promised Adam and Eve that He would send the Messiah even before the details of the "curse" were unfolded (see Genesis 3:15). They are given hope immediately, and are given another statement by God to *believe*. They are trusted with an area in which to demonstrate their belief of a promise. Yes, the promise is for something in the future, but the demonstration of their belief that God has spoken truth is something possible to them in *their* moment of history.

Yes, there will be thorns, thirst, sickness, and signs of death in all that will surround us. But if we *believe* what God has said, there is hope, hope singing through with a music that eases the pain. Hope that promises, "This isn't the end; there is something ahead. Things can be put back together again someday." We need now really to *believe God*, and act upon that belief.[1]

For Further Reading: Psalm 14, Proverbs 6, Mark 6

PRAYER

Dear Father, thank You for giving me "true truth," truth that corresponds to the way things really are, truth that is consistent with Your holy and loving character, truth that is absolute instead of relative, truth that applies to every problem, condition or situation. Thank You for explaining in the Bible what is wrong with Your good creation, how the choices we make affect real history, and what You intend to do to restore all things through the Messiah, Your Son, Jesus Christ. Help me to be firm in my Christian beliefs and act upon those beliefs with faith and hope in You and Your ultimate victory over Satan and evil. In Jesus' name, Amen.

[1] From *Christianity Is Jewish*, pp. 26, 27, 32-36.

PERSONAL NOTES

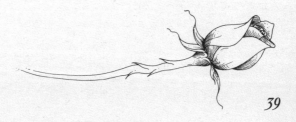

SEVEN

*"In him [the Word–Jesus Christ]
was life, and that life was the
light of men. The light shines in
the darkness, but the darkness
has not understood it. There
came a man who was sent from
God; his name was John. He
came as a witness to testify
concerning that light, so that
through him all men might
believe."*

John 1:4-7

Light and Darkness

*G*od speaks to us of "light" and "dark" to help us to understand that we can make such terrible mistakes about what the world is, what the universe is, who we are ourselves, whether there is any life after we die, whether there is a place called heaven. We can make such terrible mistakes about whether God made the world or whether it came by chance. We can make such terrible mistakes about whom to believe, and just believe lies instead of the truth. God tells us that believing lies and making such mistakes about life is like sitting in dark darkness. Then He says that because people are in such dark darkness, one of three Persons, God the Son, came to be born as a baby, to grow up to teach and live so that people would have light to see and understand what mistakes they had made.

John did not talk about himself. He even called himself a "voice of one calling in the wilderness" (Luke 3:4)! Constantly he told people what terrible mistakes they had made, and what sinners they were in their rebellion against what is *true,* and against God who really exists. John told them that a Savior was coming to save them from the results of all this sin and rebellion. John told people that a "light" was coming to lighten their darkness, and to guide their feet into the true path. John told people the *truth*.

All this happened about two thousand years ago. Now it is history. But it is important to us because it is true history. You are a person. I am a person. We are people who have been born into the world, and we are alive today in this time of history. We need to know how we "fit in." We need to know about the past, and we need to know about what is coming in the future, but we need to know what we are meant to do right now. One thing we are meant to do is to give *light* to others sitting in darkness.

We need to be sure we are not making more darkness in the world. We need to be sure what we are saying is *true*

truth. We need to *know* the Person who is "light." And we need to tell other people during the time we are alive that Jesus, who is light, *did* come, and *is* coming again. We need to *understand* as Mary understood (when the angel Gabriel told her that she would be the mother of the Messiah) and *believe* as Mary believed when she declared, "I am the Lord's servant. May it be to me as you have said" (Luke 1:38). We need to believe that these things about the Messiah are true, and act on that basis.

Eve believed Satan's lie was true. Mary believed what Gabriel told her was true, so she said "Yes," she would do what God was asking her to do, so that people could come back to God. What are we supposed to believe and do? We are to believe that the Bible is *true.* Then we are to come into God's family and sit in the light all the time. That is, when we are born into God's family by believing what He tells us in the Bible about Himself, and by accepting what Jesus came to do for us, we are children of light. We are supposed to get our ideas and our understanding from *Him* so we will not have fuzzy, dark, foggy ideas, but *truth.*[1]

For Further Reading: Psalm 36, Proverbs 7, Mark 7

PRAYER

Dear God, thank You for sending Your Son, Jesus, to be the light, the love, the truth of my life. Thank You for sending Him to live and die in my behalf, and for the sins of the world. Help me to grow in the light and come to a deeper knowledge of You and the truth so I can share truth instead of darkness with my fellowmen. Strengthen the Church in word and spirit so we might be faithful to the truth, and faithful witnesses to every generation that is desperately seeking for the way and the life that comes only from You. Amen.

[1] From *Everybody Can Know,* pp. 25, 26.

PERSONAL NOTES

EIGHT

*"For God so loved the world that
he gave his one and only Son,
that whoever believes in him
shall not perish but have eternal
life. For God did not send his
Son into the world to condemn
the world, but to save the world
through him."*

John 3:16, 17

God, the Giver

We are told that God loved the world so much that He gave His only Son—so that anyone who would believe in Him (that means anyone who would believe what He said in words, and also who would believe that what He did was for them, too) would have everlasting life. What a gift! The first part of the gift is that the Trinity agreed to be separated for a time, so that Jesus could be born, and live and teach and help people to know about Him, and then *die* so that *anyone* who would believe Him could live.

The second part of the gift is that as Jesus died in the place of anyone who believes in Him, then He gives His righteousness in place of their sins. It is as if we had a dirty cloth around our shoulders, covering us with filth and rags, and then someone came along with a snowy white tablecloth and said, "Look, I'll take the dirty cloth, and cover you with this sparkling white cloth." The *gift* of the white cloth is *real* because we are told that whoever believes and accepts what Jesus came to do for him has his sins taken away, and is covered with righteousness (that means the good things Jesus did). Then on top of all that He gives us everlasting life. Everlasting is for ever and ever. He promises us that His gift is a wonderful life ahead of us!

When someone loves you very much and gives you a gift that cost them a lot, not just money but a lot of time, you would hurt that person very much if you just kicked the gift and said, "I don't believe you love me." Just think for a while of how God feels when people turn and kick away His gift.

God is a Person, and He feels, as well as thinks and acts. How do you think God feels when people just say, "I don't believe God loves people," or "I don't believe God is even there at all"? We ought to spend more time telling God how much *we* appreciate *Him,* and ask Him to help us make other people *understand* how great and wonderful

and loving He is. He is our Father, when we have come to be His children, and we ought to tell our Father how much we love Him, as well as tell other people what a wonderful Father He is! You see, God really does love *people*, and He really *is* love. Because God is holy and perfectly just, sin needs to be punished. Jesus paid for His gift by taking the punishment we deserve upon Himself. Jesus loved us enough to die in our place.

Today lots of people are teaching that there is no such thing as truth at all, or that if something seems true today, it won't be true tomorrow. You see, this is Satan's special lie today, and so since all of you will meet some people who believe nothing is true, or will read books, or hear TV programs that say this, it is more important than ever to know not only that there *is* truth, but to know what the truth *is*. That is why it is important for families to read together what God says in His written Word, the Bible.[1]

For Further Reading: Psalm 23, Proverbs 8, Mark 8

PRAYER

Dear Father, thank You for loving me, even me, a person who, along with the rest of the world, has lived a life of sin and rebellion against You. I am a part of the world, and You love the world, and gave Jesus to save the world. You promised that those who believe in Him, in His words and finished work, will be saved and know experientially and personally Your love now and throughout eternity. I rejoice in knowing You, my God and Savior. I love You for the gift of Jesus Christ, who was willing to pay the terrible price of death and separation within the Trinity that I, along with all who believe, might be cleansed from all unrighteousness. Thank You for the clean white garment that You have given me to wear in heaven. Help me to share this truth with others that I might lead them out of the darkness and into the light. Amen.

[1] From *Everybody Can Know,* pp. 35-39.

PERSONAL NOTES

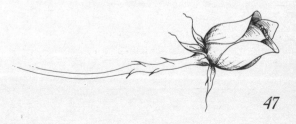

NINE

"There is more rejoicing in heaven over one sinner who repents than over ninety-nine righteous persons who do not need to repent."

Luke 15:7b

Rejoicing in Heaven

*T*he compassion of God and the compassion of the angels is so very real that they rejoice over every single one of the lost people who are found. That really is exciting! There is not one person so small, so poor, so uneducated, so uninteresting, that the angels are not excited and glad when he or she becomes a child of God by believing.

If you ever feel that nobody loves you, nobody cares about you, nobody finds you interesting, or fun to be with, that you don't matter to anybody, then remember this–Jesus told stories of a little lost sheep and of a tiny coin, not worth much in the world's eyes, to show that in the eyes of people in *heaven* no matter how insignificant we feel, we matter enough to bring excitement, joy, a real celebration right there in heaven itself!

The Bible teaches us a lot about the fatherliness of God. We are told that God is a Father to the fatherless (see Psalm 68:5). He will be a Father to people whose parents have died, or whose parents have deserted them. Then we find in Psalm 103:13, 14, "As a father has compassion on his children, so the Lord has compassion on those who fear him; for he knows how we are formed, he remembers that we are dust." That is exciting, because God is telling us that He is like the sort of a father who is kind and pities his children when they are dusty and dirty. Did you ever get dressed up for a picnic, or a family dinner, or to go to church on a Sunday, or to be taken to a concert, and then fall by accident into the dust and dirt? Maybe you were doing something you had been told not to do, but you didn't mean to get dirty! You meant to stay clean. You say you are sorry, and a kind father or mother washes you, dusts you off, and understands you, realizing that you are really sorry and forgiving you.

God says He doesn't forget that we are weak, sinful

creatures. He remembers that we are pretty dusty people, and He pities us. He is ready to wash us and clean us and forgive us when we fall. Just before that, the Psalmist had said, "as far as the east is from the west, so far has he removed our transgressions from us" (Psalm 103:12). This is as far as you *can* be removed from something! God is able to do this because Jesus died to take the punishment we deserve. God does not have to spoil His holiness by loving us that way. He can wash away our "dust." We don't have to ever be afraid of bringing people to our Father God, and of feeling ashamed of His love or of His faithfulness. His love is real, and far greater than that of any earthly father. But to experience His fatherliness, to come to know Him as Father, people must come to Him believing, and accept what He has prepared. So often people say, "I don't think God is loving," but they have never become His children, so He is not their Father. No one knows a father the way his own children know him.[1]

For Further Reading: Psalm 68, Proverbs 9, Mark 9

PRAYER

Dear God, what a joy to learn that my repenting from sin and coming to You with the empty hands of faith to receive the free and gracious gift of forgiveness brought real joy to You in the giving, and rejoicing in heaven by the angels. To imagine that I could make You happy, and that You were really saddened about my rebellion because You really cared for me personally! How blind I have been to You, Your love and compassion, because I have measured Your love by my own selfishness and self-centered spirit. Forgive me for the low and unworthy views I had of You. Lead me further by the light of Your presence. Oh, how I love to reach up my hand to place it in Yours and to be led by You in many marvelous ways, even as a child loves and trusts his father wherever they go together. Help me to share with others Your fatherly compassion: I know that You will never turn anyone away, for Jesus' sake. Amen.

[1] From *Everybody Can Know*, pp. 250, 251.

PERSONAL NOTES

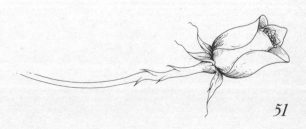

TEN

"Be kind and compassionate to one another, forgiving each other, just as in Christ God forgave you."

Ephesians 4:32

The Personal Family

*H*uman relationships are taking place whether or not anyone stops to label them. Good or bad human relationships and constructive or destructive human relationships take place at every level of life. Whether people treat people as human beings or machines, people are treating people in *some* way. Whether people treat everyone as having importance, dignity, significance, or whether people treat others on a sliding scale of importance–everyone is reacting to other people in some way. Human relationships start at birth and continue to death, whether or not anyone consciously thinks about it. Adults have been teaching children lessons of how to treat other people, in devastatingly horrible ways or in Biblically right ways, whether or not they have ever thought of themselves as teachers. Teaching takes place by example, every minute of every day for every human being.

A family is a formation center for human relationships. The family is the place where the deep understanding that people are significant, important, worthwhile, with a purpose in life, should be learned at an early age. The family is the place where children should learn that human beings have been made in the image of God and are therefore very special in the universe.

The Bible tells of the things which children should be learning at an early age in order to find out how human beings are to treat other human beings–whether they are in the personal family, in God's Family, friends, neighbors, or enemies. God gives every basic teaching, and guidance by example is supposed to be in line with what the Bible teaches. Can parents be perfect? Of course not. Can brothers and sisters be perfect? Of course not. Children should learn very early that we are all sinners and we all fall into times of misbehaving. They should know that adults don't carry out what they should, in keeping with what the Bible

teaches them to have as a basic rule of behavior. Children should know that mistakes are made and that parents fall into sin at times. Apologies should be made to small children by parents. The understanding of what an apology is and what forgiveness is should be a two-way street from the very beginning.

Pretending perfection immediately teaches falseness and rationalization of mistakes as the very first lessons taught. The Biblical teachings should be given and discussed with day-by-day pointing out of where one or another teaching can be practical, and where we may have acted contrary to the Bible. Reality in the area of difficulties in human relationships must be lived in daily experiences. The importance of "putting first things first" in human relationships should also be experienced together, as well as talked about. The understanding of how to deal with and live with human beings takes a lifetime, the fact that progress is to be expected should give a feeling of excitement to the whole relationship within the family, which will naturally spread out beyond the little family to touch other people.[1]

For Further Reading: Psalm 25, Proverbs 10, Mark 10

PRAYER

Dear Father, thank You for adopting me and making me a child in Your Family. Thank You for giving me the basic teachings I need to be a good parent to children, and thank You for being the example of the Perfect Father in Your Word. Help me to be a good parent by word and deed within Your Family, the Church, because there are many who have only one parent or none at all. Lead me by Your Spirit to those who need me, and help me to fulfill every obligation to those who need my immediate love and care, my personal family. Today, I pray also for the many outside Your Family, who need to know You as their Father through Christ. Amen.

[1] From *What Is a Family?*, pp. 68-70.

PERSONAL NOTES

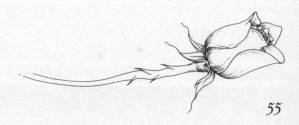

ELEVEN

*"My command is this: Love each
other as I have loved you.
Greater love has no one than
this, that one lay down his life
for his friends."*
                              John 15:12, 13

Learning Love

*T*he family is the place where loyalty, dependability, trustworthiness, compassion, sensitivity to others, thoughtfulness, and unselfishness are supposed to have their roots. Someone must take the initiative and use imagination to intentionally teach these things.

There should be family discussion about the centrality of growing relationships being more important than individual points one wants to get across. Criticism of each other may be very necessary at times, but there must be encouraged sensitivity to the fact that the whole point of communication is to have a growing relationship come forth.

Compassion and understanding of what *another* person needs comes through having been cared for. Anyone who has had the comfort of a little pot of tea, some cookies or toast, or a cup of coffee and some cheese and crackers, or a glass of milk and some fruit–just when he was feeling "down" in the midst of a project–then knows how to do those same things for someone else. A family is the place where this kind of care should be so frequently given that it becomes natural to think of the needs of other people.

Love is one of the basic commands which the Bible gives us concerning human relationships. Husbands are to love their wives. Christians are to love each other. People who are in the Family of the Lord are to love those who are not believers. Love is the basic ingredient of human relationships which is meant to be taught in the family. The family is the formation center for knowing how to love, how to express love, and what love is all about. We should be expressing love for each other verbally, and not be too embarrassed to say, "I love you, mother–I love you, dad–I love you, son," so that children grow up in a place where love is freely expressed, and becomes a perfectly normal thing to verbalize, just as "What a gorgeous sunset!" is

normal to talk about. Day-by-day living in the midst of an outpouring of examples of love is needed through months and years, if love is to be a basic part of the "warp and woof" of a person.

Love isn't just a kind of soft feeling, a thrill of honeysuckle fragrance while being kissed on a June night! Love isn't just happiness in ideal situations with everything going according to daydreams of family life or married life or parent-child closeness and confidences. Love has *work* to do! Hard and sacrificial work—going on when it would be easy to be provoked and think evil. Love takes imagination and the balance of putting first things first to be taught to the young pupils in their formative years.

Can human love be perfect? No, but it is meant to be worked at through the years, and it is meant to portray something within the family of the love of God for His Family. What is a family? A formation center for human relationships—worth fighting for, worth calling a career, worth the dignity of hard work.[1]

For Further Reading: Psalm 113, Proverbs 11, Mark 11

PRAYER

Dear God, thank You for my family, my personal family, some of whom are with You in heaven and some of whom are yet to make their journey homeward. I am who I am today because of Your love and teaching, and also because of the love and teaching of others: of those whose example commended their teaching. I have but few "spiritual fathers and mothers," and I thank You for them! I pray that You will help me to be the "right" spiritual parent to others, and I accept the responsibilities that might entail for months if not years. With the breakdown in personal families all about us, forgive me for any damage I might have caused in the lives of those in my personal family, and help them to forgive me, that we might yet learn the way of reconciliation through faith and loyalty to Your Son Jesus Christ. Amen.

[1] From *What Is a Family?*, pp. 83, 82, 86, 88-92.

PERSONAL NOTES

TWELVE

"To the Jews who had believed him, Jesus said, 'If you hold to my teaching, you are really my disciples. Then you will know the truth, and the truth will set you free.'"

John 8:31, 32

The Flag of Truth

*T*he primary place for the flag of truth to be handed on (as in a relay race) is in the family. The truth was meant to be given from generation to generation. If those who knew God and who had so very much to tell about Him had always been faithful, and had always stuck to the commands or the rules of the relay, there would have been no gaps. Each generation would have learned from the one before. Fathers and mothers were to tell sons and daughters. There was supposed to be a perpetual relay of truth without a break. The gaps in the world's history and in geographic generations of families came because of the refusal to pass on the truth—as a flag in a race.

The first family which suffered was Cain's family, as he belligerently brought his destructive piece of creative art and called it the right manner of worshiping God. What Cain handed to his children was *false!* You can picture Cain as the one who first dropped the flag and opted out of the true race, picking up something false to pass on, running away from rather than toward the goal! And a long line of children followed him. We live not to ourselves; we affect other people. Cain did. Rebellious Israelites did, when they followed the gods of the Canaanites.

Jesus cautions against false prophets, telling us that even some who do miracles in "the name of the Lord" are not true but false (see Matthew 7:22; 24:11), just as those were who put "the name of Jehovah" on the golden calf and brought their children out to dance around in an orgy of false worship (see Exodus 32 and 1 Kings 12). Just the name *God,* or the name *Jesus* is not enough. The name can be printed on a false flag, and the race can be running off at an angle, completely in the wrong direction.

The truth of the existence and the character of God is to be made known to the children and the children's children. We are responsible for our children and for our

grandchildren, for our nieces and nephews and our grand-nieces and grandnephews. That they may know *what?* The wonder of who God is, what God has done, what God has said, and what He has meant to those doing the telling. There must be some reality to relate, some true under-standing of God to pass down.

Our God is perfect in His gentleness, and is the One who says He will never fail His children nor forsake them. To fear Him means to fall flat on our faces in adoration. His greatness and love are beyond anything a human being can really understand, and we need to have for Him a feeling beyond that which we have for any human being, a feeling that makes us want to worship and be respectful. This One who is the Creator is to be marveled at, and as we walk and talk with our children, the wonders of His creation should be pointed out.

God's direct Word comes to us—consider your place in the family as central, as part of the "relay." Don't let a gap come because of *you*. Don't take the beauty of the family life—and the reality of being able to hand down true truth to one more generation—as a light thing. It is direct disobe-dience to God to *not* make known His truth.[1]

For Further Reading: Psalm 31, Proverbs 12, Mark 12

PRAYER

Dear Father God, Creator and Sustainer of life, the God who created us as one family in all the earth only to have that family relationship destroyed by Satan's evil tempta-tions and people following the wrong "father," help me to teach others the truth about You, and the truth of how anyone can become a member of Your Family through believing in Jesus Christ and what He has done for them by His death. Help me to know Your power in my life more experientially on a day-to-day basis, so that I am actually able to live in the supernatural world the Bible speaks of, so I can pass on to others Your hope for them through Your Spirit. Amen.

[1] From *What Is a Family?*, pp. 121-123, 132.

PERSONAL NOTES

THIRTEEN

"Do not be afraid of those who kill the body but cannot kill the soul. Rather, be afraid of the one who can destroy both soul and body in hell."

Matthew 10:28

Passing on Pollution

*P*olluted food and drinking water can be deceptive to the point that poison can be taken into the body without recognizing its presence. A prolonged time of taking poison into the body could be unnoticed if there were no people pointing out the dangers or testing the contents of the food and water. Death can be a result of the illnesses which result from polluted food and water.

But there is a pollution more to be feared than polluted beauty, polluted swimming water, and ruined sand castles—more to be feared than polluted air, dangerous drinking water, poisoned food. The most dangerous pollution of all is the pollution of true truth, the pollution of the absolute Word of God, the pollution of the Bible.

Insidiously, there is a dangerous pollution going on, sometimes with delicate deception. The music and the light through the stained glass seem the same. Phrases seem the same. Only a little is removed: a word there, a meaning somewhere else. This portion is deleted from history and changed into myth or parable. That portion is turned away from as unimportant, open to question. The early part of Genesis is treated with a shrug, and the reality of God's speaking in the Epistles is dismissed with a phrase attributing what is being taught only to a man who is writing. *Infallibility* is a word that becomes suddenly an embarrassment, and Satan whispers, "Did God really say?"—over and over again in different tones of voice and with fresh sneers, as he speaks *not through a serpent* but through pastors, professors, teachers who lend themselves to Satan's twisting of the Word of God. As Satan polluted the verbalized spoken teaching of God to the first man and woman, so he has continued to pollute the written Word, the Bible, from one moment of history to another.

One disastrous way in which pollution of the Bible takes place is when people no longer teach as *true* the areas

of the Bible that deal with history and science, but leave people with a floating religiosity.

Poisoned translations, poisoned teaching, poisoned writing, poisoned preaching, poisoned commentaries, and poisoned Sunday-school lessons take the pure Word of God and pollute it so that people are "breathing, eating, and drinking" polluted spiritual air, food, and water. As Jesus warned, the resulting death is eternal, not merely a shortening of this life. We are told that God has spoken, and we are meant to have His Word in a pure form.

Jesus Christ is the Bread of Life and the Water of Life. He is to be our atmosphere as we live in His presence. How? We are told that by abiding in Him, and having His word abide in us, we are prepared to be in His presence, ready for communication. Jesus prays in John 17:17: "Sanctify them by the truth; your word is truth," as He intercedes for us. But there are clear warnings that false prophets, unfaithful shepherds, and pastors who "scatter my flock" are to be avoided and not allowed to pollute the direct Word of God to us.

Can't we see that it has never been different? The Word of God is pure, it is true, it doesn't change—but there has been no time in history when someone has not been deceived by Satan and then stepped into the place of trying to pollute God's Word for others so that they would be destroyed unawares.[1]

For Further Reading: Psalm 2, Proverbs 13, Mark 13

PRAYER

Thank You, dear Father, for Your Word that purifies my life as I read it in the presence of Jesus Christ, and as the Holy Spirit interprets it and applies it for me. Protect me from polluted teachings regarding Your Word. I pray now that Your Holy Spirit would blow blaring trumpets and flash red lights when I am tempted to doubt Your Word or be led to a wrong understanding. For Jesus' sake, Amen.

[1] From *A Way of Seeing*, pp. 32-34.

PERSONAL NOTES

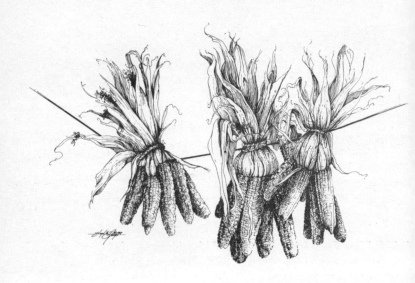

FOURTEEN

"Oh, how I love your law! I
meditate on it all day long.
Your commands make me wiser
than my enemies, for they are
ever with me. I have more
insight than all my teachers, for
I meditate on your statutes."
Psalm 119:97-99

"Meditation" or *Meditation?*

We hear a lot about meditation these days. People learn eagerly to sit in just the right position—toes curled up over their thighs, hands at rest in the lotus position, palms up, shoulders relaxed, breathing deeply, pulling in their abdomens, exhaling in exactly the proper rhythm. "Meditation." Some learn to slow down their heartbeat and triumphantly announce that it came to such a slow rate it was negligible. Mystical, cloudy, floating, unreal—separated from earthly sequence of logical thought, separated from understanding and answers to questions, separated from verbalized explanations—modern meditation drifts in ebb and flow with no defining framework. Blurred, misty, with no sharp lines.

What is the word *meditation* supposed to mean to us, as those who have come into communication with the Living God through the One Way He has opened up into His presence? What does the Bible teach us—born-again children in the Family of the Living God—about meditation?

Christians need no special position in which to put the body. Their meditation takes place all the day, during the time in which normal daily life is being lived. Here is no empty-minded, no slowed-down pulse—but a mind filled with the content of God's law: *Oh, how I love your law! I meditate on it all day long.* God's *law* is the full verbalized richness of the Scripture's explanation of the commands of God. Oh, how I love the Scriptures, the true Word of God, as I read it and think about it and come to fresh understanding day by day. Never do I come to the end of the possibility of meditating upon *that.* As I dwell in conscious thought, the seeds of God's law and God's teaching burst and send forth shoots of green understanding that I can put into words of my own. All the day long, as I walk in fields or city streets, as I sit at the typewriter or make a bed with fresh sheets, as I converse with professors or tiny

eager three-year-olds with endless questions, I can meditate upon the law, the Word of God which I have learned.
This meditation has a base, a changeless base which is as
meaningful as it was centuries ago–and is true.

I can have more understanding than my enemies or my
teachers by meditating upon the testimonies of God! The
Bible has enough content to give us understanding which is
complete in being true. What we meditate on in the Bible
can give us understanding beyond whatever of man's
knowledge we are being taught which may cut across the
Word of God.

Doing God's will, action based on God's teaching, will
follow after a person meditates–hour by hour, day by day,
year by year–upon that which God has carefully given and
protected so that it might be available to anyone.

Is there a difference? Is there danger in trying out the
wrong kind of meditation? Yes, there is danger. Satan's
traps are sharp steel which tear the flesh of those who pull
away! *Both* kinds of meditation cannot take place in one
portion of time. One kind drives out the other! Which
meditation will we have? How precious is our time?[1]

For Further Reading: Psalm 19, Proverbs 14, Mark 14

PRAYER

*Dear Father, thank You for speaking to me in Your Word,
because now I have concrete truth and reality upon
which to think as I fulfill my daily obligations. I thank You
that I can spend quiet times to read the Bible and memo-
rize verses to plant in my mind to give me direction as I
work or play, worship or teach. Help me to defend myself
and others when we are tempted to practice meditation
"techniques" built on a false base of Eastern mysticism or
ideas of a god who has not spoken verbally or communi-
cated ideas to think about and live by and share to guide
others to truth and reality. Help me to pray to You with an
understanding of who You are and of how to pray based
on Your truth, for Jesus' sake. Amen.*

[1] From *A Way of Seeing*, pp. 35-38.

PERSONAL NOTES

FIFTEEN

*"Love the Lord your God with
all your heart and with all your
soul and with all your mind."*
Matthew 22:37

True Love

*L*ove without reason is sometimes pictured as a meeting of personalities in some mystical blending of baseless emotion. The intellect is put on the other side of a high gray stone wall–where a chilly dull atmosphere is contrasted to the riot of colored flowers and warm sun-drenched grasses on the "emotion" side of the dividing wall. One is given an impression of needing to make a choice between "mind" and "heart," as if to choose one is to deny the other. Love is thought of as so delicate a wisp of cloud that it will be blown away by any wind of verbalized reason.

Is love there? Is it not there? Shhh–don't ask. The very *asking* may drive it away. Jump into some experience with your eyes shut. Close the eyes of your mind and feel–feel–feel. Don't define. Don't verbalize any reason why. The stark use of intellect will nullify the reality of love.

Is this true to what exists? What about human love which is so limited and imperfect and yet which can grow and deepen through the years? How does it grow? It grows through verbalization and deepening understanding which comes from coming to *know* the other person. In a human relationship the other person is never perfect, so there are weaknesses and faults which could hurt or destroy the love if dwelt upon. If one discovers a new reason to admire, enjoy, and be stimulated by the other person, one would do well to verbalize this discovery.

Concrete reasons for loving another human being not only need to be expressed to that person, but will also help the person who is doing the verbalizing. Dwelling in one's mind on logical reasons for love does not diminish the feelings of love, but increases them. Making new discoveries of qualities in the other person's character, through recent things he or she has done, gives increased reality in the area of *knowing* the person. Love will grow as reasons

for love are discovered, thought about, dwelt upon in the mind, expressed verbally, and remembered.

The question is asked: "How can I experience love for God? I want a flood of warm love for Him, but He seems so far away, and I feel nothing." Is the answer to be one of urging each other to wait for a mystical, spiritual experience during which we will be plunged into a riot of color and sunlight on the "emotion side of the wall"? Are we to put away intellect and logic?

How can we experience a growing love for God? By discovering logical, reasonable, understandable reasons for loving Him. We can constantly verbalize our discoveries and express our love to impress upon our memories the reasons we have for loving God. "Oh, God, how I love You for letting people come to know Jesus personally day by day. Thank You for supplying our need for food–and for adding the roses yesterday."

Love for God increases as the reasons for love are verbalized, spoken aloud, written on paper, considered in the mind, dwelt upon in the wakeful hours in the night. "Love the Lord your God with all your mind" is a command that increases love when we attempt to follow it.[1]

For Further Reading: Psalm 17, Proverbs 15, Mark 15

PRAYER

Dear God, I love You for being the God You are. I love You for creating this beautiful world I live in, with beautiful creatures and other human beings to keep me company. I love You for redeeming a great many people through the gift of Your Son, and I love You for the hope You give me in Your Word that Your creation will someday be restored. I love You for meeting my daily needs, and for casting out all my worries through the Holy Spirit's application of Your Word to my concerns. Help me to love You more and more as I discover new reasons for rejoicing in my knowledge of You. Amen.

[1] From *A Way of Seeing*, pp. 53-55.

PERSONAL NOTES

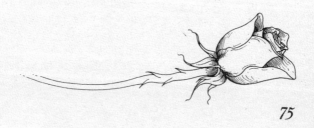

SIXTEEN

"We sent Timothy, who is our brother and God's fellow worker in spreading the gospel of Christ, to strengthen and encourage you in your faith, so that no one would be unsettled by these trials. You know quite well that we were destined for them. In fact, when we were with you, we kept telling you that we would be persecuted. And it turned out that way, as you well know."

1 Thessalonians 3:2-4

Why Must We Suffer?

*A*ffliction must be recognized as something we all need to deal with. There is no place to go for a vacation from the abnormality of the universe, from the effects of the Fall upon every area of life, and from the conflict of the ages. Persecution and affliction are a *normal* part of the Christian life. We need not be surprised or ashamed when our work, our family, our church, or our individual person is hit by some form of affliction. Satan does not fight against himself. So when those in the midst of false religions seem to be having an easier time than Christians, it should not be surprising. The criterion of living a growing, fruitful Christian life in a close walk with the Lord is neither to be "abased" nor to "abound." Both situations present temptations, but both can be places of victory. We are too easily turned toward thinking of what we can "get" in the way of happiness by being a Christian, and fail to remember a conviction and willingness to be used by God at tremendous cost.

We cannot compare our own pattern to someone else's to discover whether or not we are in the Lord's will. God has individual and very diverse plans for the lives of His children, and Satan's attempts to turn us aside are also diverse. Poverty can be an attack, but so can affluence. Hardship can be an attack, but so can ease. And when we face the death of a loved one, the attempt to twist us into bitterness can be an attack, but so can be a false covering up of sorrow.

Tremendous victory is only possible in the face of a tremendous battle. Our desire should be to help each other find victory in hidden places and "overcome him [Satan] by the blood of the Lamb" in very practical moment-by-moment happenings in our day-to-day lives.

We do not live in a Moslem, fatalistic universe. The infinite, personal Living God has done what our minds

cannot grasp. If we could understand all that God understands, we would no longer be finite and human. To demand this is rebellion against remaining in our own place as His creatures, akin to Lucifer's demanding equality with God. We are to bow to the *truth* which God has given us, with the amount of explanation He has given us. We need to be willing to let God be God, and to stay in our place as human beings. It is not necessary for us to say something like: "It was God who sent the terrorists into that building and chose my husband to be the first one shot, riddled with seven bullets, and thrown down the stairs." God does not ask us to place any such explanation upon a situation in which Satan's emissaries are striking out against the work of the Lord in His servants. The death of martyrs must not be placed anywhere but where it belongs: in the battle by which Satan is trying to stamp out the spread of true truth.

There is a battle going on that is real. History is taking place. This is not a puppet show, but a cause-and-effect history. We must acknowledge that we can't understand everything, but that we do have much help and comfort in the Bible. God is sovereign and all-powerful, and the victory is His.[1]

For Further Reading: Psalm 22, Proverbs 16, Mark 16

PRAYER

Dear Jesus, give me the strength to overcome the trials, temptations, afflictions, and persecutions that I face daily. Whether these involve being abased or in abounding, I thank You that I have been called to take a part in the "battle of the heavenlies." Give me wisdom from Your Word to encourage others in the victory that comes through faith in You and Your shed blood. Amen.

[1] From *Affliction*, pp. 28, 29, 26, 27.

PERSONAL NOTES

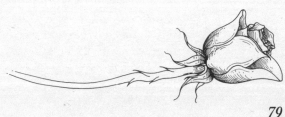

SEVENTEEN

*"He said, 'Surely they are my
people, sons who will not be
false to me'; and so he became
their Savior. In all their distress
he too was distressed, and the
angel of his presence saved
them. In his love and mercy he
redeemed them; he lifted them
up and carried them all the
days of old. Yet they rebelled
and grieved his Holy Spirit."*
Isaiah 63:8-10

The Affliction of God

We are told something that makes the battle clearer to us. The words are directly from Jesus, as He spoke to Saul on the Damascus road: "I am Jesus, whom you are persecuting" (Acts 9:5). Jesus is saying that Saul's persecution of Christians is actually a direct persecution of Him, Jesus. It is the counterpart of "whatever you did for one of the least of these brothers of mine, you did for me" (Matthew 25:40).

It is possible to persecute and afflict the Lord through the persecution and affliction of His people. The battle is fought in this way, as Satan tries to fight against God and to destroy the love of His people for Him. Satan is not only trying to make Christians bitter and complaining against God; he is trying to hurt God directly. We have a piece of information from Isaiah that God means us to have, to help our understanding. It fits in with "why do you persecute me . . . I am Jesus, whom you are persecuting." Isaiah speaks of the loving-kindness of the Lord:

> *"He said, 'Surely they are my*
> *people, sons who will not be false*
> *to me'; and so he became their*
> *Savior. In all their distress he too*
> *was distressed, and the angel of*
> *his presence saved them. In his*
> *love and mercy he redeemed them;*
> *he lifted them up and carried*
> *them all the days of old."*

This is not simply a statement of the fact that the Lord feels our sorrows and afflictions in loving concern, but it tells us also that the thrusts of Satan which come against us hit Him in some very real way. What is going on is beyond our complete comprehension, but we are meant to have a real measure of understanding to give us courage to go on.

Our personal afflictions involve the Living God; the only way in which Satan can persecute or afflict God is through attacking the people of God. The only way we can have personal victory in the midst of these flying arrows raining down on us is to call upon the Lord for help. It is His strength, supplied to us in our weakness, which makes victory after victory possible.

There *is* something to say when people ask, "Why?" or feel, in the midst of their struggles with an affliction, as if no one else had ever had this particular combination of things before. There is no pat answer or suitable phrase—but there is the reality of history to consider, as well as the absolute fairness of the Word of God in the examples He lets us look into. We have the reassurance, time after time, that our particular combination of characteristics is really unique, because we are individual personalities, not puppets or parts of a machine. It helps us to hear about other Christians in pain, difficulty, persecution, and affliction, because we then can recognize that in our own struggles we are not alone in history. We are surrounded by those who are a veritable "cloud of witnesses" who can encourage us (see Hebrews 11 and 12). They can help, not because they had perfect lives with shining successes and joys following one another like a bubbling stream through flower-filled fields—but because they, too, have discovered something about the diversity of meaning to be found in affliction and the bittersweet possibilities of victory.[1]

For Further Reading: Psalm 100, Proverbs 17. Ephesians 1

PRAYER

Dear Father, when I complain about my afflictions, remind me that every attack is really an attack against You that hurts us both. Remind me through Your Spirit and Word that I can call upon You in trouble, and You will be there to give us real victory for Jesus' sake. Amen.

[1] From *Affliction*, pp. 36, 37.

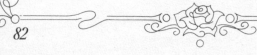

PERSONAL NOTES

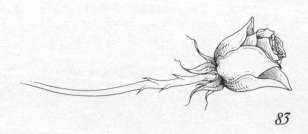

EIGHTEEN

"But we have this treasure in jars of clay to show that this all-surpassing power is from God and not from us. We are hard pressed on every side, but not crushed; perplexed, but not in despair; persecuted, but not abandoned; struck down, but not destroyed. We always carry around in our body the death of Jesus, so that the life of Jesus may also be revealed in our body."

2 Corinthians 4:7-10

The Victory Through Death

*R*ead *slowly and think carefully.* The death of Jesus on the cross was to give three distinct kinds of victory to each one who believes in Him. His death was sufficient for complete victory. First, when a person accepts Christ as his or her Savior—after sufficient understanding of the reality of God's existence (and of what true guilt means before such a God) and what the death of Christ on the cross accomplished—that person has *victory over the penalty of sin.* There will be no penalty to pay. Christ's death produced perfect victory for each one who believes on Him, and the penalty is wiped out. Second (this is really the third victory chronologically), there is *victory over the presence of sin.* One day every one of us will be glorified. This is absolute and certain after we have been justified through believing in Christ. The death of Christ brought forth a victory over what Satan had destroyed in the Garden of Eden. The extent of this victory is so glorious that we may be sure of not only being in heaven and having eternal life, but of being separated entirely from the presence of sin. There is also a *day-by-day, moment-by-moment victory* which Christ died to make possible—a most important one in the continual battle by Satan against God. This third kind of victory is meant to take place over and over again in the period of time we are still in the land of the living. The death of Christ on the cross was sufficient to provide a victory that was complete. Christ's death has opened the way to us to be immediately forgiven and justified when we accept Him as Savior. His death assures us of immediate entrance into heaven whenever we are "absent from the body." His death, however, was also to give the possibility of victory over Satan in this present day-by-day life. One of Satan's great campaigns against God is in the area of trying to break down our trust of God. We have seen it in Job,

and we know from the Book of Revelation that Satan is, has been, and will be doing that "day and night."

I believe that there is to be an historic fulfilling of proof that the death of Christ *was* sufficient for every kind of victory needed to make the reality complete. There will be no individual in heaven who *perfectly fulfilled,* moment-by-moment, a constant trust and love of God. Each one of us falls into Satan's traps from time to time, some more frequently than others. However, I believe that there will be no type of affliction or suffering that someone has not lived through with victory supplied on the basis of the shedding of the blood of Christ. I believe that "They overcame him by the blood of the Lamb and by the word of their testimony," and will be demonstrated as having included a fantastic diversity of "overcomings" throughout history (Revelation 12:11). It seems to me that the "cup of victory" will be complete.

There is titanic meaning and purpose in our individual afflictions, since the particular one Satan is hitting us with today has not been lived through before at any time in history—nor will be again. We can have a part on God's side of the heavenly battle, bringing joy to God and defeat to Satan. We can whisper, whatever the circumstances, "God, I don't understand, but I love You and I trust You. Don't let me flinch; don't let me let You down in this area of the battle."[1]

For Further Reading: Psalm 27, Proverbs 18, Ephesians 2

PRAYER

Dear Jesus, thank You for the victories You have won for me by Your death upon the cross. I thank You that I have the assurance of sins forgiven and life after death. Help me to have daily victory over sin and Satan. Amen.

[1] From *Affliction,* pp. 76-78.

PERSONAL NOTES

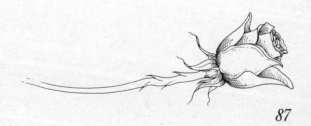

NINETEEN

"You shall have no other gods before me."

Exodus 20:3

Why? Why? Why?

When you, when we, when our children, when friends question, Why? Why? Why? concerning suffering and affliction and troubles, be sensitive to the fine line that divides grief and sorrow and frustration from bitterness that may be planted as a bad weed to grow and crush out love and worship. Pray for yourself and for all the ones for whom you are responsible, in your own generation, but also in the next generation. Ask for God's help. He alone knows what part of the shock is due to the cause-and-effect history flowing from the Fall, and what part is due to a direct attack of Satan, as in Job, and what part is to be used by Him to bring forth someone to a fantastic place of refinement, as silver is refined.

So often we do not know the source of our affliction. Pray, communicate, weep before Him, explain to Him that you are confused, ask Him for help in your reactions, actions, words, emotions, and ask that He give His strength in your weakness. Pray that this time may not be wasted, but may bring Satan's defeat, *whatever* part he has, and may bring forth something wonderful to God's glory.

Satan constantly sends his darts against Christians so they may turn to other gods. May we not dabble in anything that even smells of the occult, or of Eastern religions, or of transcendental meditation, or of mixtures of religion with diets or religion with anything that detracts from putting God first, even if it uses Christian language and calls itself Christian. Something else mixed in that may seem innocent in itself can slide into God's first place. *Help me to recognize the danger signals, O Lord. In this twentieth century give me discernment when I turn on the television and courage to turn it right off again. In this twentieth century give me courage to judge what I read, whether in newspapers or books, by Your Word. Help me to realize that many things are clamoring to turn my love*

away from You. Teach me what true fear of You and love for You mean when translated into my everyday life.

We can have a Bible in our hands, read, study, meditate, talk to the Lord about it, ask for further understanding, consistently look for help in "doing" rather than just "hearing" His Word. And we can have, whether as children, or as uneducated older people, the possibility of knowing more, understanding more, of what really is truth, what really is right, what really is the answer to Who am I? and What will fulfill me? than any of our brilliant professors who do not love God's law. The democracy of being under God's instruction, being under God's direction, being under God's commandments, being under God's verbalized explanations is a democracy like nothing on earth. Each person can come directly to the Master of the Universe, the King of Kings, the General of Generals and receive an audience.

Out of love for God flows love for other people, bringing forth action based on that love. Not putting other gods before the one true God, and truly loving Him with all our hearts and minds and souls and with all our strength is not a passive life of sitting in an ivory tower. It is an active life, as James shows, filled with positive action that has a base. Faith, James tells us, is dead faith if it is not accompanied by action. He tells us that Abraham's "faith and his actions were working together, and his faith was made complete by what he did" (James 2:22).[1]

For Further Reading: Psalm 45, Proverbs 19, Ephesians 3

PRAYER

Dear Father, I submit myself to You totally, because I love You, because You deserve my submission, and because You demand my total, undivided loyalty to You above all others. Help me to discern right from wrong and truth from error, then give me the courage and strength to do the right and proclaim the truth for the sake of Your Kingdom and honor, and for the sake of the gospel message. Amen.

[1] From *Lifelines,* pp. 42, 21, 43.

PERSONAL NOTES

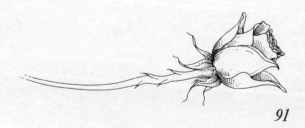

TWENTY

*"Dear children, keep yourselves
from idols."*

1 John 5:21

Turning From, Turning To

When I was a little girl my mother would often say to me, "Edith, I know just who you've been playing with today." She knew because I had become something like the other little girl, whichever one it was, enough like her that the girl could be identified by my changed accent, my mannerisms, and other telltale changes. Children often copy other children quite unconsciously. So do adults. We are affected by the people we spend time with, in one way or another. God makes clear to us that not only is it sin to bow down to idols and worship or serve them, but that there is an effect which follows very definitely. People who worship idols become like them. Sometimes it is possible to identify someone's religion or philosophy just by the look of that person, as well as by the actions and conversation.

Many twentieth-century people are turning away from God with great superiority and pride. The turning to a terrific variety of idols and false gods, old and new man-made religions, is amazing in this period of "modern" men and women. People feel liberated when they turn from God the Creator and His laws, even while they are allowing handcuffs to be put on their wrists as they become bound in Satan worship, Eastern religions, cults with a great diversity of origins, occult practices, and now a deluge of women goddesses restored from Greek times, and added to by modern inventions of new goddesses. Our universities are a hotbed of "sophisticated" new religions, even though they are only old pagan idol worship dressed in a new purple. Many old practices such as abortion and infanticide, once thought of as a part of pagan religions and acceptable only to people who worshiped idols made by men's hands, have now come back in a flood. The turning *away* from God is always a turning *to* replacements.

Added to turning away from loving God and worshiping Him is the turning away from going *to* Him for help.

Human beings cannot get along without seeking advice, help, counsel, wisdom, direction, because in this fallen world, where so many things go wrong, they need to turn to "someone higher." The only One higher is God in His perfect wisdom, might, power, knowledge, love. People need to turn to God for help. God says, "Ask of Me" over and over again. But many do not listen. They turn instead to idols and mediums and spiritists, to all manner of promised supernatural help, outside God. There is no "neutral" person or persons to whom to go. If one is not going to the true and living God for help from what is called "the other world," one is going to the Devil or demons.

When people turn away from idols and turn to God, it is a complete turning *from* the false *to* the true. There has to be a complete turning *away*, as well as a turning *to*. The danger today, as in any other day in history, is an attempt to hold on to something of false worship of idols, of meditating in an Eastern way, of sitting cross-legged in partial adoration of the sun, of some false way of getting help in making decisions through fortune-tellers or astrology.

Don't forget: when you run *away*, you also run *to*. When you run away from false gods, there is Someone waiting to receive you. Jesus says, "Come unto me." Remember that invitation when you are being laughed at, taunted, pulled in the other direction. This invitation to come *to* the throne of grace is especially connected with the fact that Jesus has gone through that *same* temptation and therefore that He will understand.[1]

For Further Reading: Psalm 79, Proverbs 20, Ephesians 4

PRAYER

Dear Jesus, I am running to You again right now, and I will continue to do this moment-by-moment for the strength I need to stand for You and with You in a world that is trying to pull me from You. Thank You for never failing me, and thank You for Your Word that encourages me daily. Amen.

[1] From *Lifelines*, pp. 49, 46-48, 52, 58.

PERSONAL NOTES

TWENTY-ONE

*"The word of the Lord came to
me: 'Son of man, prophesy
against the prophets of Israel
who are now prophesying. Say
to those who prophesy out of
their own imagination: "Hear
the word of the Lord! This is
what the Sovereign Lord says:
Woe to the foolish prophets who
follow their own spirit and have
seen nothing!" ' "*

Ezekiel 13:1-4

Naming the Name

*I*t is extremely easy to put blots on other people's repu-
tations by misrepresenting them. It is much worse to
misrepresent God, to decide what His messages and directions are to other people in practical and specific things
such as the use of time, money, talent, energy, possessions,
and so on. To double-check ourselves we need to stop and
ask, "Is this a forgery? Or is this really something that has
come from God?" God's signature is on the Bible, His
Word. We need to pray daily that we be kept from temptation, kept from the temptation to forge His signature in a
way that would be a terrible misuse of His name. It is not a
light thing to use God's name, even if it seems to be a
"spiritual" use of His name. To use God's name to back up
one's own ideas, or to use His name in exercising authority
over other people who should be coming directly to Him
themselves, is a breaking of the commandment not to misuse His name.

Years ago someone very close to me was working for a
big denominational mission board. Though not a Christian
at that time, this girl was a skillful writer and had among
her other work various articles to be included in the mission magazine month by month. She often wondered
whether her writings, which were written completely from
a Marxist viewpoint, would be deleted from the magazine,
but the editor liked her stuff very much, and only cau-
tioned from time to time, "Be sure to put enough 'Lord' in
it to satisfy the evangelicals." Later, this same girl writer
heard a prominent church leader come into a back room
after a speech and stridently ask the staff who had heard
him on the loudspeaker, "Well, did I put enough 'Lord' in
it to satisfy all the little old ladies?"

To use the name of the Lord to "satisfy little old ladies"
or to "satisfy the evangelicals" can in no way be called
anything but a misuse of His precious and holy name. The

same lips that pray "Hallowed be thy name" render that declaration meaningless when they go on to talk about using the name of the Lord to fool people as to the content of articles, sermons, or lectures. The only comparison I can think of is the use of the word "democratic" sprinkled liberally in names of rallies and seminars for Communistic teaching.

Taking credit for what the Lord is doing, putting one's own name on another person's work, is another way of misusing the Lord's name. To take someone else's painting, statue, or short story and to sign your own name is plagiarism. The people to whom the living God is their Heavenly Father should be incensed when His work and all His creation is attributed to other names. It is an insult to His name to give God's praise to *chance,* to sign "chance" to all God's creation.

We can misuse the Lord's name by saying over and over again, "Praise the Lord," while our minds are totally occupied with other things. Or if our mouths are expressing devotion to the Lord by merely repeating words over and over again with no real thought or involvement of the whole person, we are in danger of vain repetition, of babbling like pagans, of misusing the name of the Lord.[1]

For Further Reading: Psalm 97, Proverbs 21, Ephesians 5

PRAYER

Dear Father, I never want to be guilty of misusing Your name. As I think of these examples of common misuse, I pray that You will protect me from using any of them. I pray that You will give me greater insight into ways that Your name is being misused today, so that I will not be tricked by others who use Your name for their purposes. Help me to be bold, if I am called to defend Your holy name. In Jesus' name I pray. Amen.

[1] From *Lifelines,* pp. 72-76.

PERSONAL NOTES

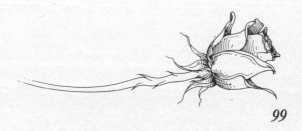

TWENTY-TWO

*"All Scripture is God-breathed
and is useful for teaching,
rebuking, correcting and
training in righteousness."*
2 Timothy 3:16

Penetrating Continuity

*T*he Bible is a very concise book, with complete continuity and containing all we need to know to understand the basic questions of life. It gives us the history we could not know, had not God chosen to reveal it to us. It gives us an account that "makes sense." It goes on to tell us as much about what God expects of us as we can handle. It also pulls back a curtain on the giant stage of the future, for a brief moment, so that we may glimpse something of the wonder of what is ahead. We are not left with a fear that nothing will ever change. We are promised that perfection is something we are yet to experience.

God made people to be able to have a continuity of truth and a relationship with Himself that would not have had to be broken. Continuity is a part of who human beings are.

The fabric of the Bible is woven with unmistakable threads of continuity which bring understanding of the centrally important truths to the diverse minds of human beings who have read or heard these truths over all periods of history and in every geographical location in the world. The Bible is not a book of broken bits and pieces, isolated stories and parables that make a collection of religious tales. The Bible presents true truth, truth that is unchanging, truth that fits in with what exists, truth that answers the questions of life.

How spectacular is God's utter fairness in communicating to the human beings who had turned away from His truth to the lie of Satan, when he tempted them in the Garden. How wonderfully awesome is the *hope* of a Savior that God set forth without delay to those two who must have known depression after their tragically wrong choice.

God is utterly fair. He gave a very complete book for us to read and reread.

It is possible to read the Bible with no human help and

have the marvel of the continuity and wonder of truth become crystal clear. My husband, Francis Schaeffer (as I wrote in detail in my book *The Tapestry*), thought he had found the answers to all his philosophic questions in the Bible as the very first person ever to do so! He accepted the Lamb as his Savior without human help while he was only seventeen years old.

Dr. Hans Rookmaaker, a leading art critic and former professor of art history in the Free University of Amsterdam, had nothing but the Bible to read during his imprisonment in solitary confinement during the war (he was Dutch, being held by the Germans). During that reading he saw the marvel of the answers . . . the continuity . . . the truth . . . the awesome wonder that the key was there in the Bible. It made sense. It gave the answers that nothing else did. He believed there in the prison. Neither prison bars, in Hans Rookmaaker's case, nor theologically liberal preaching, in Francis Schaeffer's, could shut out the clarity of the light which is the truth. Truth can penetrate a great variety of darknesses! Hope.

The warning at the end of the Bible is that nothing is to be taken away from this Book, and nothing is to be added. The continuity of truth is not to be added to nor subtracted from. God's Word is truth. No wonder it is attacked by the enemy![1]

For Further Reading: Psalm 56, Proverbs 22, Ephesians 6

PRAYER

Dear Father, thank You for the beauty of the Bible. Not only do Your words correspond to reality, to what is really true and real in history, but Your words correlate with one another as a complete system of thought, a complete system of salvation, with a logical continuity that is truly overwhelming to my finite mind. I thank You for Your Holy Spirit who reveals this beauty to me in a saving sense for my redemption and eternal life. Amen.

[1] From *Common Sense Christian Living*, pp. 53, 54, 58, 61, 63.

PERSONAL NOTES

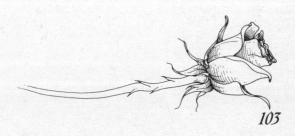

TWENTY-THREE

"I have loved you with an everlasting love; I have drawn you with lovingkindness."

Jeremiah 31:3

Absolutely Perfect

*T*here is a factor in our relationship with God that is totally different from our relationship with husband or wife, mother or father, children, sisters or brothers, cousins, aunts, grandparents, friends, fellow workers, neighbors, church members, and so on. That factor is that God is perfect. Our Heavenly Father, our Friend and Shepherd; our Intercessor Jesus Christ; our Comforter the Holy Spirit are each perfect!

God's side of His relationship with us is absolutely perfect. He is so tremendous in His infiniteness and His diversity that we will never get to the end of coming to know Him. But the gradual progress of knowing God will never be on the same level as knowing a finite, limited, everchanging human being. God tells us that He does not change. He will be tomorrow as He was yesterday. We can depend on Him to be faithful, reliable, trustworthy. He has said He understands us. We are told that the promises He made centuries ago are just as true today—not just true in the academic sense of truth, but true to you and me personally. His truth makes a difference to our present lives, as well as to our part and place in eternity.

Let's consider for a moment our relationship with God, and the factors needed to make it a growing reality, since our side of that relationship is imperfect. Continuity of any relationship needs verbalized expression of love and trust, as well as actions that show forth love in a variety of practical ways day by day.

God has carefully given us His Word, which expresses His love clearly, so that we can reassure ourselves constantly as we read. When we read, "God so loved the world" (John 3:16), it is not meant to be impersonal, but it is in reality a precious verbalization to each of us personally. God carefully expresses His love so that there is no shadow of doubt. We are meant to take His Word as true to us

personally and actually bask in His verbalized love. When we read Jeremiah 31:3, we are meant to respond not only inwardly, but also with a verbalized response. When we read in 1 John 4:10, "This is love; not that we loved God, but that he loved us and sent his Son as an atoning sacrifice for our sins," we are meant to accept that love as if we were reading God's letter written just to us, each one personally. God has carried out His love in action, in the most perfect way. But He also has verbalized His love in words we may read over and over again, sing, hear in our brains. For this reason, we are meant to read the Bible frequently so that we may have the communication of the continuity of God's love in the midst of a broken world full of hate.

How can I help my love for God my Father, Jesus my Savior and Lord, the Holy Spirit my Comforter, to become more real, to grow with a constant growth? One necessary means of growth is verbalization of that love and trust in thoughtful and constant words. Our own ears need to hear our own voices telling God we love and appreciate Him. Our own minds need to think of the endless reasons why we love God, but those reasons need to be put into words and spoken.

Constantly during the day we need to verbalize to the Lord our expressions of love, dwelling on the reasons for that love, whether it is the titanic reason of His providing eternal life, or the recognition of the wonder of His design of the first snowdrop or violet found in the woods in spring.[1]

For Further Reading: Psalm 18, Proverbs 23, Colossians 1

PRAYER

Dear Father, thank You for loving me not only in deed but also in word. Thank You for not leaving me to my own imaginations or reflections about whether there is or is not a God of love. Thank You for doing all that You do from love, and then verbalizing to me about a close and lasting personal relationship through Jesus. Amen.

[1] From *Common Sense Christian Living*, pp. 71-73.

PERSONAL NOTES

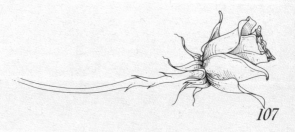

TWENTY-FOUR

*"Be joyful always; pray
continually; give thanks in all
circumstances, for this is God's
will for you in Christ Jesus."*
                    1 Thessalonians 5:16-18

Conscientious Prayer

*M*y first observation of perfectly natural and conscientious prayer came when I was a very little girl in Shanghai. One morning I went skipping along beside Dr. Hoste, at that time the director of the China Inland Mission (he had followed Hudson Taylor). He didn't turn me away, but simply said, "Edith, I am praying now, but you may come along if you wish."

I walked with him a number of times, holding his hand and being very quiet and impressed as he prayed aloud. It was his custom to walk when he prayed, and he counted it his first responsibility for the mission to pray four hours a day. He prayed for each missionary in the China Inland Mission, and for each of their children by name. He had the list with him, and he went through it. It was not just a recitation of names; he cared about each person and knew something of their needs. He felt this was his work.

"All right, walk with me and pray," he would say in his peculiarly high voice. The impression that penetrates my memory is the respect I received for the *work* of prayer. I know it meant more than any series of lectures in later life could mean.

I know a farmer who used to be a L'Abri worker. He writes that he now prays as he works on his tractor. He carries the prayer list with its page of verses and another page of requests on the L'Abri day of prayer each week. In this sense he is still a L'Abri worker. Even as his hours are spent raising quantities of mint, his hours are also being used to affect what is going on thousands of miles away.

Whether it is the farmer in his tractor, portioning out time for prayer, or the head of a mission who considers prayer more important than paperwork or talking to a number of people waiting to see him—there is no rule or measuring stick by which you can say, "So much prayer gives so much spiritual result." This is not the way it is;

many people could never take four hours every day to pray, nor do they ever have quiet time riding miles on a tractor.

However, in your lifetime there should be some whole days, or blocks of time, that you take to spend alone with the Lord, just as you do with some member of your family or a close friend you haven't seen for a long time. You say, "Let's just not take time eating today! We are going to sit down and have a really uninterrupted conversation together. I haven't seen you for so long; there is a lot of catching up to do."

From time to time we have to do that with the Living God, our Heavenly Father, the Master of the Universe. This is something that cannot take place in snatched moments, and that is an unhindered time of progressive conversation.

I would recommend that you take a longer period of time to communicate with the Lord, to read His word, to carefully bring things to Him concerning yourself and your own need, and to take sufficient time to thank Him for Himself. There is a cumulative freedom of communication as you read and pray for a variety of needs in other people's lives as well as in your own.

As the time goes on, five or six hours or more, there is a sense of quietness, like having been in the home of a very calm person in a location separated from your own pressures. Pressures are removed as time goes on. The time is really like being in a protected country place. Nothing else is like it in my own life. You will have to try such a time to know what I'm talking about.[1]

For Further Reading: Psalm 65, Proverbs 24, Colossians 2

PRAYER

Dear Father, if I don't have the time or the longing to spend time with You, give me the time and give me the longing. Through an extended period of time with You, inspire me to make this the norm of my Christian life. Amen.

[1] From *Common Sense Christian Living*, pp. 211, 212.

PERSONAL NOTES

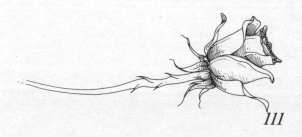

TWENTY-FIVE

*"But who am I, and who are my
people, that we should be able
to give as generously as this?
Everything comes from you, and
we have given you only what
comes from your hand."*

1 Chronicles 29:14

Leftover Beauty

*O*ne can look at the great artwork of an unbelieving person and worship the God who made people in His image to be able to create such magnificent works of art. One can look at an outstanding bridge being built and bow before the Creator God who made that engineer, even if the engineer himself knows nothing about God. One can listen to music with a satisfaction and a thrill, full of thanksgiving for it–being appreciative of the composer and at the same time whispering an acknowledgment to the fantastic God of Creation who created not only the universe, but beings with creative brains and abilities!

Two things have been true since the Fall. First, human beings are horrible, capable of treating other human beings with cruelty. We do this not only to our enemies, but to family members, and even to our own children. The Bible speaks of the ways of peace not being known to those who have turned away from God and have exchanged the truth of God for a lie, and who are full of all kinds of immorality, deceit, self-seeking, and shedding of blood. We are distressed when we hear reports of increased crime, of new ways of self-destruction, and of the destruction of others with a stream of diverse ways of evil treatment of human beings. How long has it been since these people who do these things were in their mother's arms or being fed in a highchair? Where do such awful people come from in such a short space of time since birth? Where does the low view of life come from during so few years?

Second, human beings are wonderful in their acts of compassion for starving people half the world away, in their bravery that is so often amazing, in their creativity–composing and performing exquisite music, making diverse and beautiful instruments, designing space shuttles, making computers, building hospitals and an array of fascinating art objects and diverse things, in their study and prac-

tice of medicine and their work to save lives and give relief to suffering people. Human beings are really astonishing in what they can do spontaneously or learn to do in such short lifetimes, whether in exploring unknown parts of the world or in swinging by their teeth from a high circus rope! Human beings are astounding in that they require so few years from birth to being an astronaut, or from the high-chair to conducting a great orchestra.

The reality behind the first fact is the historic Fall. "Man fell from his first estate." The Fall has brought death in every sphere of life.

The reality behind the second fact is that human beings were made in the image of God and are finite and limited but are personalities with purpose and meaning in history and with capabilities to be unfolded. "Leftover beauty"–beauty and capabilities and potential that have not been wiped out–gives glimpses of some of the sheer wonder that has been lost. People have a reason to treat people differently if they understand that all human beings are made in the image of God and have different bits of "leftover beauty."

Francis Bacon wrote, "Man, by the Fall, fell at once from his state of innocence and from his kingship over creation. Both of these misfortunes, however, can even in this life be in some part repaired; the former by religion and faith, the latter by the arts and sciences."

Restoration and perfect solution are ahead.[1]

For Further Reading: Psalm 144, Proverbs 25, Colossians 3

PRAYER

Dear Father, thank You for creating everyone in Your image so that we can appreciate the wonderful creativity of one another. Help us to place our creativity under Your Lordship, that You might anoint and bless our efforts to responsibly bring forth real beauty, not ugliness and further destruction, in the world You have made. Amen.

[1] From *Forever Music*, pp. 112-115.

PERSONAL NOTES

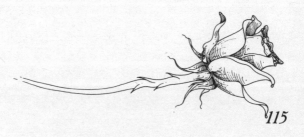

TWENTY-SIX

"Sanctify them by the truth;
your word is truth."

John 17:17

Ideas Come First

Franz's father had Jews as his closest friends. One day he said to his boy, "Look, son, Hitler is sending Jews to some kind of work camps. It is an awful thing. I don't know where they are going, but I know that this is the end of Germany. It's the end of Germany, boy. 'He who touches My people touches the apple of My eye' (see Zechariah 2:7-9). That's God speaking, and the Jews are His people. Mother has prepared sandwiches and other food for my friend Ben the butcher who is in the station. Go. Take this food. Go and get it to him somehow."

They assumed the Jews would be made to work very hard in camps. That was a horror to Franz Mohr's family, and a fearful thing that was resulting from totalitarian rule. The gas chambers and all that was going on was not known to them during that time.

Where did Hitler come from? Or Lenin? Or Mao? Or Stalin? Or Amin? What about the Berlin Wall? What about Afghanistan?

What is the cause that brings an effect into the place where it is seen, smelled, touched, heard, felt? How do actions come?

In the mind. Just as creativity is in the mind first, so devastating destruction is in the mind first. Violence is in the mind first—from *ideas*.

Ideas come first.

Ideas matter.

Ideas give birth to action—good or bad.

Ideas give people their world view.

Ideas push people into heroism.

Ideas drive people into vandalism.

Ideas are meant to be handed down from generation to generation. One generation is responsible for the next—whoever is doing the planting of ideas. The parents, or teachers, or professors in universities may live a life of ac-

tions based on what is left over from some other teaching. That is, it is quite possible for people to have an ethic that does not belong to what they are teaching the next generation. They are then surprised and even dismayed when the next generation, their own pupils, begins carrying out in action what they have been given in the realm of ideas.

People do open doors down for following generations—down into the depths of despair for thinking young people, down into drastic action for others. Suicide follows for some.

The people who bear responsibility for the actions taken in different periods of history are those who inject ideas into the minds of the young, one way or another.

Many people today think that no educated person could possibly believe that there is any unchanging standard for ethics and morals. Rather, since everything is in a state of flux, and since everything is relative, it would be impossible to say that it is "wrong" to kill people. Hitler chose to rid his kingdom, as he was thinking of it, of Jewish people and of those who were weak or in mental institutions because he made up his own rules based upon what was acceptable to himself.

If God exists; if Scripture, the Bible, is the Word of God; if the explanation of the Fall gives us a background of the Devil and also of the abnormality of the world, then it is easy to see that relativism is the kind of lie you would expect from Lucifer who declared to Adam and Eve, "You will not surely die."[1]

For Further Reading: Psalm 99, Proverbs 26, Colossians 4

PRAYER

Dear Father, teach me the truth of Scripture so I can be cleansed from false and destructive ideas and actions, and help me to teach this truth to others so we can make a difference for good in the coming generations for the sake of Jesus' Kingdom. Protect us from ideas that kill and destroy when applied. Show us how Your Word speaks to the whole of life and all our needs and concerns. Amen.

[1] From *Forever Music,* pp. 160-165.

PERSONAL NOTES

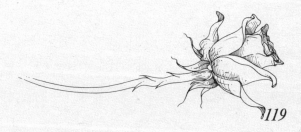

TWENTY-SEVEN

*"I will refine them like silver
and test them like gold. They
will call on my name and I will
answer them; I will say, 'They
are my people,' and they will
say, 'The Lord is our God.'"*

Zechariah 13:9

The Master Technician

When people put themselves into the hands of the Master Technician–that is, God their Savior and Creator–they may expect constant help. We go "out of tune," or become "harsh" so quickly. We need to come to the Master to be "tuned" with His strength put into us, substituted for our weakness. We are told of being refined as silver.

Even as pianos need constant tuning and regulating–not only when young and raw, but all through their careers of being used for brilliant concerts–so people who are being used as "instruments of righteousness"–or, in other words, living creative, fruitful lives–need constant refreshing, "tuning." It came into my mind that receiving God's strength in our weakness as we call out to Him for help is very similar to a piano receiving new brilliance when the hammers are made harder with the proper juice or made softer and more mellow with some pricks of the needle-like instrument. Our "Master Technician," God, knows just what we need so that we are at times more "brilliant" for something we need to do, or more "mellow" or "soft" for other compositions we need to have come through us!

Jeremiah felt he had no "voice" with which to speak as God had asked him to speak. And God, in terms of piano technicians, "voiced" him for his difficult task of speaking with clarity.

God "voices" His children, His prophets, His creative people, to speak in various parts of history–even as a concert grand piano technician voices his instruments to bring forth compositions with clarity, according to the particular need.

Our Master Technician must continually "tune" us, "tone regulate" us, "soften" us and remove some of the "harsh notes." We need "voicing" over and over again. We need to be cleansed of what is spoiling our beauty as in-

struments as well as being given the right work suited to our capacity as instruments. We are not to try to be prepared to bring forth that which we have not been made to do. As a flute, one can never be a piano; as a French horn, one can never be a harp. On the other hand, we are never finished products. Until the Messiah returns to change us in a twinkling of an eye to be perfect, we will always need the constant help of God our Helper and Master—even as a concert grand piano needs the constant, skillful help of the master technician. God alone really knows what our capabilities are, what is in us to be brought out.

There is an admonition in the book of Romans not to think of yourself more highly than you ought to think. It is a warning to be humble. However, a balance is needed. We are to *do* what God has for us to do with His special gift of "tuning" us for our part. Jeremiah was too quick to draw back and say, "I can't do it." But God pointed out that he could indeed do "it" with His help.

Of course, no illustration fits perfectly, but it is correct to see a parallel between a concert piano needing constant regulating, and believers, the children of the Heavenly Father, needing *constant* help to be rid of harsh notes, of ugly voices, of flat responses, of too sharp a blast. We each need individual attention and cleansing of secret faults, as well as God's strength given to us moment by moment if we are going to do what we have been prepared to do![1]

For Further Reading: Psalm 12, Proverbs 27, James 1

PRAYER

Dear Creator Father, thank You for making me as I am, thank You for redeeming me through Jesus Christ, thank You for "tuning" me daily so I can be the servant You made me to be. Fill me with Your Holy Spirit, give me strength for my daily tasks, and guide me to do those things for others and myself that will be pleasing to You. Amen.

[1] From *Forever Music*, pp. 191-193, 200.

PERSONAL NOTES

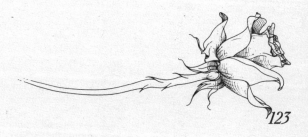

TWENTY-EIGHT

*"Blessed is the man who
perseveres under trial, because
when he has stood the test, he
will receive the crown of life
that God has promised to those
who love him."*

James 1:12

Prayer and Perseverance

*N*inety days in Europe in 1947 was a devastating time for Fran. He had real problems and struggles, and his "victories" were real too, not something to be taken for granted. It is not "spiritual" to *ignore* the scope of temptations, and never speak of them in considering a piece of work someone is being asked to do. The putting aside of our physical oneness, as well as of our talking everything over together day by day, was extremely hard on him. Added to that, the food was not only very often poor, but he very often skipped meals, he lost weight, and was ill. Added to that he had not had enough sleep at any point along the way, and sleeping in fifty-six different places in ninety days didn't help much! Travel, far more tiring than travel today, took a toll on him physically so that he came home not only exhausted, but in a condition many of us have faced after a terrific day-and-night push of work has used up all our nervous energy. He collapsed.

Never forget this . . . at any point in life, in a thousand different kinds of situations, the *answer* to the prayer, "Use me, Lord, I want to be greatly used of Thee," can be the hardest thing you have ever faced. It is the *answer* to this prayer that brings exhaustion of a variety of kinds, and that brings a cost to be paid that almost smashes you, and me. There is a cost to being "used mightily for the Lord" and there always was. Whether that cost is dying in a concentration camp, as Dr. Hoste did in China, or having a physical or nervous breakdown, the *reality* of having been used is not wiped out by the resultant cost. We are in battle, and winning a skirmish brings scars and sometimes deep wounds.

If you are raising your eyebrows in doubt of this, go back and read Paul's list of the difficulties he went through. His prison epistles were not a "breeze" for him to write, chained and without nourishing food, let alone any that

tasted good! Paul did not hide his difficulties but rather says, "We do not want you to be uninformed, brothers, about the hardships we suffered in the province of Asia" (2 Corinthians 1:8a). If he was under pressures far beyond his ability to endure, why are we so loath to mention pressures, whatever sort they may be? We do each other a terrible disservice if we end on a crescendo of glory and never mention the cost God's servants have always had woven into their piece of the battle or their section of The Tapestry.

Upon his return, Fran was required to make a report in Philadelphia. We went together, with my relieving him of all the details. He showed his slides at the banquet and gave a powerful message in his report . . . but my part of praying in the background, of caring for the arrangements and just being with him, was essential. He didn't have a breakdown, but if there had been *no one* to understand and take care of him, recognizing the needs, he could have. Does that erase the marvel of all that had happened? Not at all. But it is unrealistic to forget that until Jesus comes back again, not one of us will arrive at a place where we are no longer to be assailed from within and without.

We had been on a stepping stone that three-month period, and our lives were never going to be the same again. The next stone was soon to be put into view, and our feet were to be poised to jump over the rushing water to it . . . but for the moment we didn't realize it.[1]

For Further Reading: Psalm 139, Proverbs 28, James 2

PRAYER

Dear Jesus, forgive me for thinking that life would be easy for me and all concerned if I simply prayed, "Use me, Lord, I want to be greatly used of Thee." I commit myself to serving You fully, but be present always and give me Your strength for the battle. Amen.

---

[1] From *The Tapestry*, pp. 272, 273. I wish to thank Dallas Groten for suggesting I include these pages.

PERSONAL NOTES

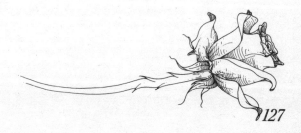

TWENTY-NINE

*"Now that you have purified
yourselves by obeying the truth
so that you have sincere love
for your brothers, love one
another deeply, from the heart.
For you have been born again,
not of perishable seed, but of
imperishable, through the living
and enduring word of God."*
1 Peter 1:22, 23

Searching and Struggling

*I*n 1951, the Schaeffer family moved to Chalet Bijou above fields on the lower side of the village in Switzerland. The hayloft, still full of hay being stored for the peasant owners, was the scene of one of the central "events" of Fran's life. He describes something of his struggles there in the Preface of his book *True Spirituality*. Before we had left Chalet des Frenes he had said to me, "Edith, I really feel torn to pieces by the lack of reality, the lack of seeing the results the Bible talks about, which should be seen in the Lord's people. I'm not talking only about people I'm working with in 'The Movement,' but I'm not satisfied with myself. It seems that the only honest thing to do is to rethink, reexamine the whole matter of Christianity. Is it true? I need to go back to my agnosticism and start at the beginning."

Pilgrim's Progress talks of the Slough of Despond, as well as Doubting Castle. Where was Fran? How long? It is impossible to analyze someone else's struggles for honesty and sincerity and certainty. It is foolish to try to copy other people, or to repeat another person's experience. Sometimes it is important for someone to walk among thorns and sharp rocks in order to post warnings, or to mark the trail with freshly painted hiking signs, indicating the best path around some hornet's nest or a precipitous cliff. It isn't necessary for everyone to set forth in the wilderness to mark his or her own trail if others have walked that way before!

The advantage of writing thirty years after the fact is that I can see something very startling now as I read hundreds of letters from people helped by the unshakable certainties Fran ended up with as he came out of that struggle to "blaze the trail" for himself, but with markings for others to follow more easily. As he says, "L'Abri would have not been possible without that time." If he hadn't had

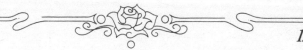

the "asbestos protection" of the honest answers to his own honest questions, he couldn't have coped with the blast of questions coming at him at times like a surge of heat from a steel furnace. He isn't giving things to other people that he has thought up as clever answers, in an academic way, for theoretical questions. He asked his own questions and discovered–and rediscovered–the answers in the Scriptures. A great deal of prayer is interspersed in his thinking–prayer asking for wisdom.

Was I so wise as to know this would be the result? No, of course not; I was scared. And when a wife or husband, a friend, a brother, a sister, mother, father, son or daughter is scared of the "searching" or the "struggle" or the "rethinking" of the other person, it is hard to know when to talk, and when simply to "intercede"–that is, to intercede by asking for God's help for the other person. It is as important to know when to keep quiet as to know when to speak clearly and courageously. Just keeping quiet can at times be the greatest work or activity of a whole period of time during which an "event" like this is going on! Surely not one of us has wisdom enough to know when to talk, and when to be quiet, without asking God for such wisdom–time after time. I can still hear the cowbells in the field in front of my little office window as I would stop typing, often during those days, open my Bible on the typewriter, and pray.[1]

For Further Reading: Psalm 4, Proverbs 29, James 3

PRAYER

Dear Father, many people around the world are going through days of struggling and searching trying to find reality, meaning, even You. Many of these people have never seen a Bible, or they do not know there is saving treasure inside Your Word. Reach them through Your servants. Amen.

[1] From *The Tapestry,* pp. 354-356.

PERSONAL NOTES

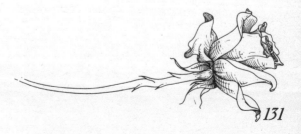

THIRTY

*"In the last days the mountain
of the Lord's temple will be
established as chief among the
mountains; it will be raised
above the hills, and all nations
will stream to it."*

Isaiah 2:2

Commitment

*F*ran thought of the name *L'Abri* (simply French for "The Shelter") as a name that would be good for our chalet, as we envisaged its work in the future. We looked back over the years in Champery, and realized that although we had not gone there for that reason, we had had a constantly increasing number of young people, and others, coming to us for spiritual help. "Let's call it *L'Abri,* and let these people know that they are welcome to come back and bring friends with them."

Then avalanches and floods descended suddenly upon us. One day, after the danger of more avalanches had ceased, I was sitting at my typewriter, feeling that "haunting question mark" along with the heaviness that went with the uncertainties ahead for the two sick children and a combination of problems that seemed to deluge us. I propped my Bible up on the keys of the typewriter, and asked God to give me the help and comfort I needed. My reading took me into the beginning of the Book of Isaiah. (Not because I opened the book haphazardly, but because that was the next portion, as I read straight through.) Now I believe the Bible is, to the spiritual life of the Christian, what warm fresh whole wheat bread is to the physical life—both nourishment and appetizing! There are also times when God speaks to some of His children in the very words of the Bible, written hundreds of years ago . . . yet seemingly written as a message for the situation of the moment.

What do I mean, "God speaks"? Does one hear a voice? I personally never have. I simply mean it in the sense one uses it concerning other printed words "speaking" to one with a special message.

Let me tell you what happened that day as I read Isaiah 2:2. My feeling was one of excitement. I read it over again, and then again . . . then reached for my pencil and wrote in the margin: "Jan. '55, promise . . . Yes, *L'Abri*."

For I had had the tremendous surge of assurance that although this had another basic meaning, it was being used by God to tell me something. I did not feel that "all nations" were literally going to come to our home for help, but I did feel that it spoke of people from many different nations coming to a house that *God* would establish for the purpose of making "His ways" known to them. I felt these people would tell others, and would say in effect, "Come . . . let us go up the mountain . . . to the house of the God of Jacob; and *He* will teach us His ways, and we will walk in His paths." It seemed to me that God was putting His hand on my shoulder in a very real way and that He was saying that there would be a work which would be His work, not ours, which man could not stop. I felt that this work was going to be *L'Abri.*

That was a moment of excitement, tying in with our feeling when we first started back across the ocean–the feeling that God was going to do something, as we wanted Him literally to take over our lives, and use us as He wanted to, not according to our own plans.

In the small measure in which we have come to put self aside, and to wait for God's direction, we have found, and will find, reality in a two-way communication with God.

There are, and always will be, many places for improvement in our struggle to be honest before God, hour by hour, day by day, month by month. This is not a life of ease, but a life of tremendous excitement, in between the struggles: excitement because of finding that we are in contact with the supernatural today.[1]

For Further Reading: Psalm 1, Proverbs 30, James 4

PRAYER

Dear Father, I commit myself to obeying Your Word under the leading of the Holy Spirit. Guide me and speak to me that I might speak to others of Your saving grace. Amen.

[1] From *L'Abri,* pp. 75-77, 206, 207.

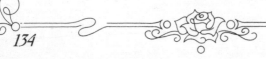

PERSONAL NOTES

THIRTY-ONE

*"As God's fellow workers we
urge you not to receive God's
grace in vain. For he says, 'In
the time of my favor I heard
you, and in the day of salvation
I helped you.' I tell you, now is
the time of God's favor, now is
the day of salvation."*
2 Corinthians 6:1, 2

Time

When we went to Switzerland right after the war, Europe still bore its scars–war-damaged buildings, and people living under stringent conditions as far as home and food went. But that which had become a deep concern for us was not the result of physical bombs which had torn up and scattered orderly *matter* into rubble, but the philosophical and theological "bombs" which had torn up and scattered faith and orderly *thinking*. It was not only that theology and philosophy were denying the existence of a personal God such as the Bible sets forth as being really *there*–that has been loudly expressed for many years–but the alarming thing was the generation growing up to be taught that one might as well not argue about what truth is, because "absolute truth" is non-existent . . . all things are "relative."

The most precious thing a human being has to give is time. There is so very little of it, after all, in a life. Minutes in an hour, hours in a day, days in a week, weeks in a year, years in a life. It all goes so swiftly! And what has been done with it? A burning zeal to do something in the realm of art, of music, of other creative fields, of science, of medicine, of exploration, of just plain living–yet how much time is there to develop in one's chosen field and to accomplish anything that makes even a smudge of a difference? When one feels one has found something far more important than how to utilize a lifetime with some purpose, when one feels one has found an open door to eternity with endless time to spend and an unending purpose to spend it *for*, when one is certain one is in communication with the Person who makes all this possible, then the burning still is there . . . but it is in a desire to *share* this certainty.

"God's guidance." "God led us." What meaningless phrases these must be to anyone who thinks there is no God; or that if there is, He is not personal and so could not

be contacted by any sort of real communication; and that if He could, He would surely not care about any such insignificant speck in the universe as one human being, and that human being's use of his hours, days and life; or if He spoke one could not understand Him anyway, as He is absolutely different.

There is *reality*. There is the certainty of the God who is there. There is the possibility of seeing that God works in space, time and history. There is the certainty of being in communication with Him rather than having some nebulous psychological crutch to enable one to bear life!

The thing about real life is that important events don't announce themselves. Trumpets don't blow, drums don't beat to let you know you are going to meet the most important person you've ever met, or read the most important thing you are ever going to read, or have the most important conversation you are ever going to have, or spend the most important week you are ever going to spend. Usually something that is going to change your whole life is a memory before you can stop and be impressed about it. You don't usually have a chance to get excited about that sort of thing . . . ahead of time!

"O Sovereign Lord, you have begun to show your servant your greatness and your strong hand. For what god is there in heaven or on earth who can do the deeds and the mighty works you do?" (Deuteronomy 3:24).[1]

For Further Reading: Psalm 69, Proverbs 31, James 5

PRAYER

Dear Father God, Creator and Sustainer of all life, Redeemer and Lord, thank You for giving Your only Son to be the Savior of the world. Thank You for giving us Your time and for being patient with us while saving us from sin and its results. Empower me to share this "good news" with others as I give my life and my time through Jesus. Amen.

[1] From *L'Abri*, pp. 27-29, 226, 53.

PERSONAL NOTES

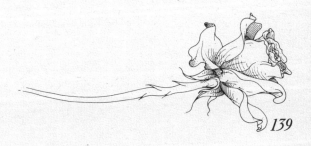

Bibliography

Schaeffer, Edith. *L'Abri*. Norfolk Press, London, 1969.

Schaeffer, Edith. *Hidden Art*. Norfolk Press, London, 1971.

Schaeffer, Edith and Francis. *Everybody Can Know*. Tyndale House Publishers, Wheaton, Il., 1973.

Schaeffer, Edith. *Christianity is Jewish*. Tyndale House Publishers, Wheaton, Il., 1975.

Schaeffer, Edith. *What is a Family?* Highland Books, Crowborough, 1983.

Schaeffer, Edith. *A Way of Seeing*. Fleming H Revell Company, Old Tappan, NJ, 1977.

Schaeffer, Edith. *Affliction*. Hodder & Stoughton, London, 1984.

Schaeffer, Edith. *The Tapestry*. World Books, Waco, Texas, 1984.

Schaeffer, Edith. *Lifelines*. Hodder & Stoughton, London, 1982.

Schaeffer, Edith. *Common Sense Christian Living*. Kingsway Publications, Eastbourne, 1985.

Schaeffer, Edith. *Forever Music*. Triangle, London, 1986.

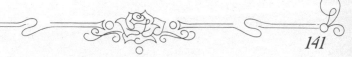

ILLUSTRATOR'S
Postscript

As you progress through the book, notice how the roses on the personal note pages gradually open up. They illustrate the spiritual unfolding process of the person who is open to God and His truth, and who allows God's truth to make a difference in personal attitudes and actions. The green leaves, called *sepals,* unfold from a tight rosebud in the first chapter to show that beginning to read about God's truth indicates an openness to receiving Him fully in our life. The Christian life involves daily spiritual growth, and by grace through faith we will reach that stage of being totally open to God in love and service to Him and our fellow human beings.

I also hope you will see and appreciate the pen and ink drawings in this book for the simple beauty of God's creation that I have tried to capture. You will sometimes find a correlation between the meaning of Edith's words and the picture illustrating the devotion. In your daily meditations, we hope you enjoy discovering what we had in mind when we selected the drawings for each chapter.

Illustrating *The Art of Life* in cooperation with L. G. Parkhurst, Lane Dennis, and Karen Mulder has brought spiritual growth into my own life. I have admired the work and words of Francis and Edith Schaeffer for many years and have tried to reflect their understanding of Christianity and art in my work, because their ideas have profoundly affected the way I work as an artist today. Edith's words in this book carry great weight, and I am deeply thankful for the opportunity to have a part in honoring her and the God who inspires her creativity as a writer.

—*Floyd E. Hosmer*